Freedom Guide

Freedom Guide

HOW TO MAKE YOUR MORTGAGE IN A WEEKEND

*7 easy steps to vacation home
rental business success*

Cathy Burch

Melrah Enterprises, LLC

Contents

The Freedom Guide is dedicated

to my beloved sister Evelyn Beasely.

She lost her battle with breast cancer the summer of 2007.

But, her life was a great victory and inspiration

to many individuals.

My sister was a gifted "techie" long before

it was popular to be a computer genius.

I'm forever grateful to her for opening my eyes

to the power of online marketing.

Special Acknowledgement

I'd be remiss not to thank my friend and mentor Mr. Howard Greenburg. As a specialist in cultivating self-generated leads, he's one of America's top salesmen. He's become one of America's top salesmen by mastering the art of becoming a friend to total strangers in less than twenty minutes. This, more importantly, is combined with an amazing skill level in closing the deal – getting a signed agreement and some form of payment. He's a highly sought after expert. I, therefore, am truly grateful to him for taking the time out of his busy schedule to teach me the skills necessary to become a top closer as an entrepreneur or in any corporate environment.

Introduction

THE *Freedom Guide* is a step-by-step guide to transforming your home (primary residence) into a successful vacation home rental business. This is an excellent opportunity for any homeowner whether your home is in foreclosure, you're experiencing financial stress in keeping up with monthly mortgage payments, or you simply want to earn additional income. In just seven simple steps, I'll show you how to turn the liability of maintaining your home into an asset that puts extra money in your pocket every month.

This proven seven-step process is guaranteed to make you money. You might wonder "How can she be so confident that this will work for me?" Because, I have personally experienced success utilizing the *Freedom Guide*. I went from having my home in foreclosure, with an auction date, to my home now paying for itself and providing me with additional monthly income.

It's amazing how moments of crisis or adversity can inspire ingenuity and creativity. Having lived in Las Vegas, Nevada, for more than twenty years, I was well aware of Las Vegas' ranking as one of the top tourist destinations in the world. Unexpectedly though, with the onset of the recent financial crisis, Las Vegas and the state of Nevada were one of the hardest hit by unemployment along with one of the highest rates of foreclosures in the country. But, for months, despite such dire economic times, I failed to realize that an amazing opportunity was staring me right in the face.

Call it luck or call it fate. Somehow, I stumbled across some life-changing information that would not only save my home from foreclosure but would provide me with an additional stream of monthly income. Now, after reaping the rewards of transforming my home into a vacation home rental business, I want to teach others how to make money using the *Freedom Guide's* simple seven-step process. All that's needed to get started is the desire to generate extra income and a willingness to put in the time and energy to set-up your home and begin implementing a marketing strategy. The rest is easy. Everything you need to know is explained in detail in this book.

I initially entered the vacation home rental business to save my home from foreclosure. But, the vacation home rental business is a $100 Billion industry with a worldwide distribution network. Thus, there are unlimited opportunities to earn money. Whether you own a home in a major tourist city like Las Vegas, Nevada or in a mid-sized city like Akron, Ohio, there is a mixture of clearly identifiable and hidden opportunities for generating revenue and making your business a profitable one.

Some rental homeowners hit the jackpot when national and international events like the Olympics, the Super Bowl or the Presidential Inauguration come to their town. They rent their home to tourists for unbelievable prices. But, you don't have to wait for a major event to be hosted in the city where you live to start your business and to begin earning additional income. You just have to develop a mindset to create those opportunities, to immediately recognize them when they become available and to seize them. With the right marketing plan and a "go-getter" attitude, the right opportunities will eventually come your way. But, you have to be prepared to take advantage of those opportunities. And, that's what the *Freedom Guide* will do. This book will not only teach you how to transform your home into a vacation rental property; it will teach you how to turn the liability of maintaining your home into an asset that puts extra money in your pocket every month. In this book, the seven simple steps have been outlined. You just have to make the choice today to seize the opportunity that will begin transforming your home and your life.

Cathy Burch

GET MOTIVATED

THE $100 billion dollar vacation rental industry has grown at a staggering rate over the last decade. Annually, more than 500 million travelers search for accommodations. And, millions of them choose to book a vacation rental home. You, too, can benefit from this trend by making your home many vacationers' next pick. Maximize the true financial potential of your property by earning enough money to pay your mortgage in a weekend.

The idea of paying your mortgage in a weekend from renting your home to vacationers probably sounds too good to be true. This is because most people are skeptical of any money making idea that sounds easy and simple to implement. But, the reality is that turning your home into a resort is not as difficult as you may think. It only takes a little motivation and follow-through on your part. The rest is clearly mapped out in the Seven Steps of the *Freedom Guide*.

The fact of the matter is that wherever there's a destination that people visit or a hotel that has regular customers, there's a market for your business as the owner of a vacation rental property. If people are traveling to the city, town, or village in which you live, then they need a place to stay. And, if the price is affordable and comparable to what an individual would pay to stay in a hotel, then most individuals would prefer to enjoy the comforts that come with renting someone's home instead of a hotel.

Vacation hot spots exist all over the globe in which cities and states thrive off of tourism. And, if you're lucky enough, owning a property in a hot spot that is not being utilized is like failing to claim a winning lottery ticket. In 30 days or less, you could be capitalizing on the asset of owning a home that exists in a primary destination of national and international travelers. Below is a list of some of the most popular national and international travel destinations and hot spots for tourism.

Vacation Hot Spots

USA	INTERNATIONAL
New York	Mexico
Nevada	Canada
Florida	US Virgin Islands
Illinois	Jamaica
California	Turks & Cacaos
North Carolina	England
South Carolina	France
Arizona	South Africa
Hawaii	Australia
Pennsylvania	New Zealand
Missouri	Japan
Alaska	China

Various Types of Vacation Rentals

You, however, don't have to live in a vacation hot spot to have a successful vacation home rental business. That's because, there's a rental market for just about every type of home. And, as we stated in the first few paragraphs of this book, "Wherever there's a destination that people visit or a hotel that has regular customers, there's a market for your business as the owner of a vacation rental property." It doesn't matter if it's a tree house in Iowa, an Igloo in Alaska, a castle in India, a teepee in Montana, a hilltop windmill in Portugal, or a cave home in Vermont. The only missing ingredient is your ability to effectively market and get the word out about your vacation rental property.

To broaden your perspective of the endless possibilities for vacation home rental, we've outlined on the following pages a summary of a wide range of homes and residences that can be converted into vacation home rental properties.

Suburban Homes

Many individuals envision the typical suburban home as one with white picket fences and a well-manicured lawn. But, not all homes on the outskirts of our big cities look or feel the same. What suburban homes do have in common, however, is an escape from city life.

Owning a suburban home is many professionals ultimate goal. Every day they commute back and forth from the busy metropolis to the world of suburbia for peace and tranquility. It's for that same reason that their homes are so marketable. Many vacationers want to experience that same feeling of escape, peace and tranquility that some suburban vacation homes offer.

Apartments/Flat

Apartments are ideal for vacation rental. They provide more immediate access to the events and activities of a major city or a college town. And, for some vacationers, they'd rather be close to the action and nightlife rather than feeling secluded.

Condominiums

A greater number of condominiums have been developed in more populated tourist areas in recent years. Some of these developments market to career driven professionals as well as retirees who are seeking vacation properties as second homes. Therefore, individuals who currently own condominiums can capitalize on the large market of potential renters.

Cabins

Many outdoor activities such as skiing, snowboarding, hiking, fishing, camping and rafting attract millions of vacationers to mountain and forest areas every year. If you own a cabin or any other type of residential property in these places, you will get bookings. Places like Lake Tahoe, Nevada, Shawnee Pennsylvania (Pocono Mountains), Big Bear California, Catskills in Upstate NY are just a few locations where homeowners can enjoy the rewards of the vacation home rental business. Wherever your cabin is located, as long as there is tourism, you can be very successful in this business.

Oceanside/Lakeside Homes

Water is a dream feature and an expensive one. Whether it's a lake, a river or an ocean, water automatically attracts visitors. Being able to secure accommodations near water is a commodity which vacationers are willing to pay top dollar.

If your home is sitting off a beach, a coastline, or a serene lake off the backdrop of mountains, you have been truly blessed. Vacationer's dream about the opportunity to wake up close to nature. And, particularly, with the increasing levels of stress that many individuals experience, serenity and tranquility are very attractive and highly marketable features.

Luxury High Rises

These properties are in high demand for rental all over the world if nothing else but for the views. However, if you want to attract guests who are willing to pay top dollar for luxury accommodations, you have to be willing to furnish your rental with the amenities and décor to which your customers are accustomed. Owning a luxury high rise that is centrally located near fine dining and high end shopping are added bonuses.

Luxury Estates

Luxury Estates appeal to the wealthy and many travelers who simply have an appetite for opulence. Whether they can afford it or not, they're willing to spend the money. If you're fortunate enough to own a Luxury Estate, you're sitting on a gold mine that will enable you to instantly increase your wealth.

Estates are very spacious and ideal for several families to jointly book a reservation at top dollar. With the total rental price being divided within the party of travelers, their dream home getaway may be less expensive than a two star hotel. But as the owner of a luxury estate, you're still guaranteed to receive top dollar for the booking. Thus, it can be a real win, win situation. The renters' are able to significantly upgrade their travel accommodations by booking as a group, and the estate owner gets to live in a mansion for almost nothing.

Specialty Homes

Vacationers taste for the unusual or out of the ordinary has its demand as well. If your home has some weird or very rare qualities, then there's a good chance that these features can be successfully marketed. Your home may offer exotic accommodations or be located in a remote location. Online marketing is the best route for these owners. There are specific portal sites that work with unique properties and advertise them as such. They tap into vacationers that are most likely to give a unique home a try.

There's an increasing demand globally for homes that are "Going Green." Because of the increase in consciousness regarding energy conservation, green homes are very popular and highly marketable. I recently watched a travel show on television that featured a home that was built out of recyclables. It doesn't matter if you have a solar-powered home, a natural gas heating system, or something as lovely as an organic garden in your backyard. There is a definite market to rent your home as a vacation rental property. You just have to begin spreading the word about your home and what it has to offer.

Specialty homes have their own unique identity and design. While the suggested staging tips that are discussed in detail in the next chapter can be used, you also want to be creative in using different approaches to match the vacation experience you are selling. For example, showcase your properties environmental assets: snowcapped mountains; rolling hills; an ocean view; a lake view; forest trees; and, sunny beaches. These are features that can emotionally hook prospective guests.

Vacation Rental vs. Traditional Bed & Breakfast

You don't have to staff a vacation rental. Renters, of course, can choose additional services for an extra cost. But, the beauty of it is that they get the keys and access to the space for a limited period of time. And, not having on-site staff is one less person to pay.

One of the most favorable things about the vacation home rental business is that you can continue to reside in your home. And, having access means having control. Renting a property in the traditional way limits your access to the property.

If your traditional renter stops paying rent, the only option you have is eviction. This is a process that takes time, money and aggravation. Meanwhile, the meter is ticking. The longer your tenant remains in your rental property, the more money you're losing each day. This is compounded by wasted time at court hearings and mounting legal fees. The vacation home rental business minimizes these types of conflicts and situations regarding the rental of your property.

The advantages of renting a room in your home also doesn't compare to vacation home rental for a number of reasons. The income you generate is not as high. Yet, you incur a greater expense in utilities. Renters typically are transient, and, therefore, may not offer a consistently stable source of additional income. You'll also lose some of your privacy while being subject to the same eviction process of a long-term tenant if future conflicts arise between you and the renter. The vacation home rental business minimizes those types of issues.

According to the "Home Away Vacation Rental Report (2010)," second home owners that utilize their homes for vacationers, earn an average of $35,000 in income. The report also states that the average property rents out over 20 weeks a year. Thus, approximately 38% of owners generate enough income to cover 75 to 100 of their mortgage. And, nearly two-thirds of owners earned enough to cover at least 50% of their mortgage.

Advantages of Vacation Home Rental vs. Hotel Rental

The best part about vacation rentals is that you can have your home pay for itself while you are still residing in it. This includes earning enough additional income for vacationers to pay for your temporary accommodations during their stay in your home.

Vacation home rental, for one, is more economical than hotel rental. And, in this tough economy, vacationers want to get more bang for their buck. Most hotel rooms in high tourism areas average two to four hundred dollars a night. The average hotel room is only 500 square feet and can only accommodate four people. A three-bedroom vacation home, however, varies from two to three hundred dollars nightly and is, on average, 1200 square feet. A vacation rental also generally has the capability of comfortably accommodating up to seven people.

Most hotel rooms rarely possess the cozy features that a home does. Whether you have a pool, a pet -friendly environment, or a child's playroom, your home's features of being economical, private and spacious are valuable incentives to vacationers.

Advantage and Appeal of Your Home to Vacationers

These are some of the factors that vacationers consider when booking a vacation rental.

1. Privacy- Some people value a private environment for their vacation.

2. No Check-In lines. Some people don't want to have to wait to check-in after traveling to their destination and

then stand in lines again to check-out. Pulling up to their destination is hassle free.

3. Keeping the party together. Groups that book vacation rentals are under one roof. This is unlike staying in hotels where they would be split up in various hotel rooms and sometimes down the hall or even in different towers. Enjoying their experience together is important to some vacationers and can be a key factor in why they select your property for their vacation.

4. Convenient Parking. Some vacationers hate having to park away from their resort in self-parking or even having to leave their car with valet. People appreciate being able to pull into the driveway near the front door.

5. Flexibility with Check-in & Check-out times. Particularly when dealing with large parties and groups, being lenient with check-in is another opportunity to offer excellent customer service. Sometimes, doing the little things that hotels' won't do for their guests can make the difference in gaining a customer's repeat business or future referral.

6. Pricing. The opportunity for vacationers to get more bang for their buck, in and of itself, makes your home very appealing. In price comparison alone, there can be as much as 50 to 60 percent in savings to the vacationer.

The numerous advantages to vacation rental are obvious. A hotel room could never be a home. But a home offers everything a hotel offers and more.

There are endless opportunities that are available for you to transform your home into a vacation rental property. And, one of the key incentives is that you can make your mortgage in a weekend. I want to reemphasize how realistic it is for you to actually pay your mortgage in a weekend. The "Common Sense Analysis Chart" on the following page further illustrates the potential income that can be earned.

Let's Do the Math

Sally Paid Her Mortgage in a Weekend

Sally has a $700 per month Mortgage.

She lives in Phoenix, Arizona.

Sally owns a 3 bedroom 1,300 square feet home.

She rents her home for $200 per night.

The Davis family from Iowa booked a reservation to stay at Sally's residence for 3 nights. The negotiated rate of payment was $200 per night for 3 nights + a $100 Cleaning Fee. Sally in one weekend earned $700 which enabled her to pay her mortgage.

Common Sense Analysis

Estimates of Nightly Vacation Rental Rates

Apartments/Condos (per night)

Studio Apt.

($150-$250) + $200 cleaning fee X 3 days = $650-$950

1 bedroom Apt

($175- $300) + $200 cleaning fee X 3 days = $725-$1,100

2 bedroom Apt

($225-$350) + $225 cleaning fee X 3 days = $900-$1,275

3 bedroom Apt

($275-$425) + $225 cleaning fee X 3 days = $1,050-$1,500

Homes (per night)

Up to 1400 sq ft

($225 – $425 + $200 cleaning fee) X 3 days = $875-1,475

1500 to 2500 sq ft

($450-$500 + $200 cleaning fee) X 3 days = $1,550-1,700

2700 to 3500 sq ft

($525-$600 + $250 cleaning fee) X 3 days = $1,825-$2,050

4000 to 5500 sq ft

($600-$750 + $275 cleaning fee) X 3 days = $2,075-$2,525

6000 to 8000 sq ft

($850-$2,500 + $450 cleaning fee) X 3 days = $3,000-$7,950

*Pricing for the following Accommodation Rates can vary at owner's discretion.

*Taxes should also be factored in your costs.

Luxury Accommodations

The same concept applies to villas, mansions and luxury high rises with regards to your rental equaling your monthly mortgage payment. Once you crunch the numbers, you'll see how easy it is to make your mortgage in a weekend through vacation home rental.

At worst, even if you don't meet your initial goal of paying your mortgage each month through vacation rentals, you'll at least be earning additional income. And, the higher your mortgage is, the more significant this becomes. Every dollar counts, especially in this economy. And, I'm certain that a few thousand or hundreds of dollars per month in additional income can help boost your family budget in a number of ways.

I hope you're beginning to see the money making opportunity that's available simply by using an asset that you already possess. But, to see the simplicity of this money making opportunity and be prepared to take action, you must have the right mindset. Purchasing this book brought you one step closer to discovering an avenue for creating greater financial freedom in your life. But, unless you follow-through, you will have squandered a great financially rewarding opportunity.

Get yourself in the right mindset. Believe that you've already won and that your financial needs will be met. If you're in foreclosure, have the courage to fight for your home. Don't give up and roll over. You fought to get the home. You now must fight to keep your home.

Focus on cultivating a mindset that you're going to do everything within your power to win. You're going to channel all of your built up frustration, anger, disappointment, despair, uncertainty, fear, and worry and turn it into one of your greatest victories. The *Freedom Guide* is one of several financial strategies that you're implementing to secure a better future for your family.

Imagine having financial abundance. Imagine having more than enough to cover your expenses and to be aggressive with long-term savings and investments. But, in order to maximize the information and strategies presented in the *Freedom Guide*, it's important that you:

1. Don't get personally attached to your home. Your immediate response to this statement is probably "How does she expect me to not be personally attached to my home? My family lives there, my belongings are in the home, and some of my fondest memories are in my home."

   I'm simply saying that you shouldn't let your pride get in the way. If you're in fear of something getting altered or broken in your home, then maybe this isn't the business for you. Things are going to get altered and things are going to be broken. Some of your items and belongings may also be stolen.

   You just have to look at it from the perspective that you can always replace what's stolen. But, if you're in financial hardship or facing foreclosure, it's going to be very difficult to buy another house if you lose the one you currently own. You're going to have more headaches trying to get banks to extend credit to you in the future.

   If you arrange your agreements properly and collect a good-sized deposit, broken and missing items will be a very costly mishap for the renter. I doubt your coffee pot is worth $500 to $1000. Your renter's know it too, which is why the deposit becomes a big deterrent.

If letting other people sleep in your bed is a very uncomfortable or awkward feeling for you, I suggest switching out the mattress. Making your mortgage in a weekend rental is worth storing your mattress in a locked area of the home and utilizing another mattress for the vacation renters. Another more feasible option is to use mattress covers. I prefer the kind you can put the entire mattress in. Protecting your mattresses for sanitary and health reasons is very important. I recommend natural probiotic products that clean, sanitize and protect. If that's your only hang up, then we've already found an easy solution. A little extra moving of the mattress is much better than tossing and turning at night wondering and worrying about how you're going to pay your mortgage.

Put your pride aside and put on your business cap. A great business opportunity is staring you right in the eyes. Remember there's always a way to get things done.

2. If you're experiencing financial hardship and possibly foreclosure of your home, then we must look at the reality of the options available to you. It's time for you to start looking at your home as the bank and the vacation home rental business as your ATM card. But, to cash in, you have to put away your skepticism, commit to reading the *Freedom Guide* in its entirety, and then begin implementing the "Seven Steps."

Are you ready for major change in your life?

Are you ready for financial prosperity?

Are you ready to experience greater financial freedom?

If the answer is "Yes," then, let's get started.

SET-UP YOUR HOME FOR BUSINESS

SETTING up your home for business is a simple process, and the cost is minimal. Besides the $24 cost to purchase this book, your main expense is the time, energy and consistent effort that you're willing to put forth to apply each to the "Seven Steps" to building and maintaining a successful business.

It's important to legalize the business. Therefore, you, first, must conduct your legal homework. This is to ensure that you're aware of and in compliance with all city, state and county requirements for legally owning and operating a vacation home rental business. There may be particular licenses that you must obtain in order to legally operate your business. If you're a member of Home Owner's Association, there may be special rules and regulations regarding renting your property. There also may be special zoning requirement or permits that are needed in the area in which you reside.

Seek legal advice from your attorney with regards to setting up the business to avoid any fines, penalties or hearings that may result from being out of compliance. This includes advice on incorporating your business. If you can't afford an attorney, there are government agencies and non-profit organizations that offer "free" initial consultation services for people who want to start their own business. Check with your local Small Business Administration (SBA) or Small Business Development Center (SBDC). Some of these agencies have retired executives and attorneys who are consultants on their staff. You can also refer to the list of agencies and non-profits in the "Toolbox."

Initially setting up your business as a sole proprietor is the most economical way to get started. Contact your local County Clerk/Recorder's Office to file a Fictitious Business Name and contact your Business License Division to apply for a Business License. However, , as soon you begin generating revenue from the business, incorporating the business should be given high priority because it provides you with additional layers of liability protection (against lawsuits). If you operate your business without incorporating, you're putting your assets at tremendous risk. There are particular advantages to incorporating in the state of Nevada. The bestselling book Nevada Edge by Cort Christie is an excellent resource for understanding corporate structure and selecting the right entity for incorporating your business. This book simplifies and easily explains what the average person perceives to be complicated.

Incorporating is not as difficult as you may think. But, working with a reputable, full service firm like Nevada Corporate Headquarters is also helpful. In addition to being experts on corporate formation, they offer sizable discounts for business owners wanting to incorporate. Log on to www.nchaffiliates.com/freedomguide/config.php. In the vacation home rental business, accidents do happen and conflicts between renters and owners may arise. Having the proper asset protection for your business will ensure longevity in this business. If you're already having difficulty making ends meet, the last thing you need is to be sued by a disgruntled guest. You're in this business to make money and to retain your assets. You don't want to put your assets at risk.

Tax Advantages

Owning a vacation rental property has many tax advantages. But, having a corporate entity or LLC in place for your business is extremely important. Depending on the type of entity you select, there are certain tax advantages available. There will be many deductions that you will be entitled to as a legitimate business owner. The IRS allows you to write-off many business expenses. Travel expenses, maintenance expenses, and advertising expenses are just some of the expenses that can be deducted. Being incorporated also projects a higher level of professionalism to your customers.

Other tax advantages of being incorporated may be tied to whether or not you have a stock portfolio. You may be eligible to utilize your stock investments as collateral to invest in real estate that, then, can be converted into ownership of a vacation rental property. Depending on the type of entity you set-up and lending programs to which you apply, you may be eligible for a loan two to three times the value of your portfolio for the purpose of vacation home investment. Check with your Broker or Investment firm to obtain more information.

Comply with all the regulations that might pertain to the business in your state and protect your business. This includes paying your taxes. The "Toolbox" has a list of all the tax websites in the U.S. This will allow you to follow-up in your home state to see their requirements.

Give Your Business an Identity

It's also important to give your business an identity. Marketing and branding image are crucial. This begins with selecting a distinctive name that people will remember and reflects the style and uniqueness of the accommodations offered by your vacation rental property. This includes selecting a name that you can cross-market with your internet marketing. My company name for example is "Desert Charm Estate." This has a good ring to it in a variety of formats including how the website address reads (www.desertcharmestate.com) and how it reads as an email address (info@ desertcharmestate.com).

Quail Estates, Bubble Hill or Hunter House are examples of other descriptive names that visually describes the property. These names also emphasize the personality and character of the vacation rental property. While these names are already taken by current business owners, they should spark some original ideas. Just remember that your business name is your trademark in cyberspace.

Your goal is for your brand to become as popular as it can be online and offline. That's why giving careful thought to the selection of your company's name is critical. There still are countless ideas for original names that will enhance your efforts to effectively market your vacation home rental. Because there are so many ways that your company name can be used to market your business, you want the name to be catchy, easy to read and easy to remember. This includes toll-free numbers like (855) FDGuide.

Now that you've legalized your business by incorporating or beginning as a sole proprietor, it's time to open a business checking account and savings account. You're ready to begin conducting business transactions. And, by having a business checking account, you'll prepare yourself to accept and deposit cash, credit cards and PayPal payments.

Insurance

CBIZ vacation rental insurance program is a great option for specialized coverage. Check out a commercial policy and an additional umbrella to see if it will give you the proper coverage and peace of mind. www.cbizspecialtyinsurance.com.

There are many variables that affect your insurance premium. For one, rates and risk factors vary depending on whether or not your vacation rental property is occupied or unoccupied. Location, weather, past claims, non-family members occupying your residence, and even the fluctuation of the stock market are other significant factors.

Your insurance premiums are also directly impacted by the

severity of natural disasters regionally and internationally (tropical storms, hurricanes, tornadoes, earthquakes, mudslides, floods, oil spills, and wildfires). Some of the most desirable vacation hotspots have been victim to these types of natural disasters. And, in a number of instances, damages from these types of natural disasters have cost insurance companies billions of dollars.

Assembling the Team

Owning and operating a vacation home rental business is a wonderful idea. But, you need a solid team around you for your idea to work and for your vision to come to life. You, first, have to remind yourself that more can be accomplished as a team than as an individual. In other words, no matter how gifted or talented you are, don't try to do everything by yourself.

Ask for help as needed. Because, over time, you're going to have to wear many hats and you can easily experience burnout. I suggest you take a moment to think of all the family and friends who may be able to assist and write each of their names on a piece of paper. Next to each person's name write the different skills they possess and tasks with which they can assist.

Next, schedule your first team meeting. The primary objective of the first team meeting is to share with the team members a clear picture of the vision and the goals you have for your business along with your plan for accomplishing them. The secondary objective is to receive a definite commitment from each team member as to how they will support you in accomplishing your goal of being a successful business owner. If they're excited about your vision and believe in it, then they'll want to contribute in any way possible. Once you've assembled your team, including what individuals will assist you with physical labor, you, then, can begin physically setting up your home.

Physical Set-Up

Many of us have a positive vacation experience that we can recall. Take a moment to reflect on one memorable vacation experience. Remember the scenery, the smells, the sounds, the colors. Each of these elements contributed to your positive vacation experience.

Most individuals, when they recall a positive vacation experience, will remember staying in a hotel. And, during your stay, it probably was the little things you noticed that made the entire experience very memorable. It may have been a piece of candy, some complimentary beverages, a welcome letter, a gift basket. Or, it may have been the courteousness and friendliness of the staff. Whatever it was that made your vacation experience memorable, you want to make every effort to ensure that your guest feel the same way you felt during your positive vacation experiences.

A positive vacation experience is what you're providing your clients who decide to book their vacation with your home resort. So, make a conscious effort to stimulate the right mood for your guests to give them a good feeling about your home. Your goal should be to make their vacation experience as memorable as possible.

Hospitality, customer service, amenities, and the upkeep of the physical environment are four critical components to ensuring that your guest's vacation experience exceeds their expectation. Your neighborhood, curb appeal, and the entry to the home also set the tone for your guests. First impressions can make or break your business. Vacationers start judging their experience at your home long before they reach the front door. They're initially attracted to your home because of the amenities it offers, the quality of the photos and the resorts proximity to major venues. But, maintaining their excitement about your property and their level of comfort requires a consistent effort in providing quality customer service.

The "Wow Factor" is what you're seeking. From the time your guests open the front door to the time of their departure, you want to reassure your guests that they made the right decision in selecting your property for their vacation rental. The curb appeal, landscaping and physical condition of your home needs to be well maintained. Your neighborhood and the entry to your home play an important role in conveying to your guests that you want them to feel comfortable and that you maintain a high standard of quality. Even with a limited budget for upgrades, you'd be surprised by the difference a couple of fresh plants or flowers can make.

"Mi casa es su casa" is how your guests should feel throughout their stay. By making your guests feel that "Your home is my home," they will want to return to your property on numerous occasions and also refer family and friends. And, you never know what other long-term benefits will result from providing your guests with a positive vacation experience. In addition to referring family, friends, and co-workers, they may want to stay for a longer period of time, possibly even for the entire summer or winter months.

Dress Up

Your pictures are the window to the positive vacation experience that you're selling. They can either pique your guests' interest or immediately kill the deal. Pictures are just as powerful in creating impactful ads. So, it's highly important that you take the time to think through and plan to photograph the best pictures of your home and the landscape of the property that will entice vacationers. Once you're certain that your pictures grab the attention of potential guests, you can feel more confident about creating an ad that will guarantee results in the form of bookings.

Your set-up is extremely important. You want to highlight the best features of your home and property. Stage furnishings in a tasteful manner while being mindful of the lighting and the angles.

Try to stick with the same set-up, colors and furnishings that you advertise. You will find that your vacationer will tell you that your home looks exactly like what they saw in your ad. Vacationers are very fickle consumers and generally don't like change. They will hold you to whatever you sell them on. So, you must be prepared to deliver by keeping your presentation consistent with your advertisement.

Use quality décor for the furnishings. And, decorate with colors that will be appealing and stimulate intrigue and greater interest. If you're on a budget, spend a day watching different television shows that feature home makeovers. These shows reveal many of the secrets that interior designers use in working with their clients. Many of these industry secrets will not only inspire your creativity. They'll save you a lot of time and money.

Theme rooms and luxury features like theatre rooms, exercise rooms, game rooms, pools, and spas should particularly be accentuated. Features in the home such as a Jacuzzi in the master bedroom or a state-of-the art kitchen not only are attractive amenities. They enable you to charge high nightly rates by catering your marketing efforts to more upscale clientele. To generate bookings, you must effectively showcase these types of features as part of your marketing efforts. Great amenities combined with a great marketing strategy will result in greater sales.

Tips for Great Pictures

Use a camera with great picture quality. If you have the money to invest, you may want to think about hiring a professional photographer to take the photos. Even with professional photos, you still need to make sure that the other elements to taking quality photos discussed in this chapter are applied. Using a digital camera is an added bonus because most digital cameras are compatible with the equipment that is used to download photos to your computer. And, at the time of purchase, they generally are already equipped with Photo Editing software.

Some printers possess photo editing software as well. Using photo editing software will enable you to quickly and easily adjust the color, sharpness and exposure of your photos. You can also crop and manipulate the angles of your photos.

You must find the best angle for taking each picture. Take photos that are shot at the best angle and show off the space, definition, décor, and furnishings at their best. Take vertical & horizontal shots.

Getting the correct lighting is key. Pay special attention to the glare of the sunlight. Your goal should be to showcase the best features and assets of each room in your home.

Take plenty of photos. You want to select from at least twenty of your best photographs. And, portal sites only allow you a limited number of photos to upload. But, you can save other photos in your archive or toolbox in case you need to show the potential guest additional photos. I can't begin to tell you how many deals I've closed only after emailing potential guests additional photos that they specifically requested.

Staging

Taking pictures is an important part of marketing your home resort. But, unless your home is properly staged, then, you will not be able to capture the qualities and features of your home resort that will be most appealing to vacationers. Every home has a personality. You want to create and capture the character and personality of each room in your home.

The goal is to create an environment that appears to be bigger, brighter, and evokes a feeling of warmth and comfort. You want your vacationer's satisfaction to be fueled by excitement and anticipation while touring and viewing each and every room. You're also trying to set a mood. And, knowing the reason that your guests are traveling offers you an additional advantage in your staging and marketing efforts.

Honeymooners, for example, may appreciate a romantic theme table for two with carefully arranged candles, chocolates and flowers. They may also enjoy a freshly prepared hot bath upon their arrival along with a trail of rose petals leading to the tub.

The type of mood you set is not limited to romantic themes. The mood can also be silly, fun, exciting, crafty or dreamy. You simply want to connect with the emotion and interests of your guests. Kids, for example, love toys. Teenagers love videos, and elderly guests love books and puzzles. Guests will appreciate the thoughtfulness, extra time and additional effort you give in catering to their special needs.

Staging the Kitchen

Kitchen and bathrooms, in particular, are thoroughly inspected by guests. Because they will be carefully scrutinized for cleanliness by vacationers, they must be shown at their best. When staging the kitchen there are small things you can do that will have a big effect.

1. Apply furniture polish or orange oil to wood cabinets to give them a renewed look.

2. Display large bowls of fruit such as shiny green apples, vibrant oranges, and juicy looking grapes.

3. Spread colorful and inviting cookbooks on the counter.

4. Strategically position polished stainless steel cooking equipment such as blenders, mixers, microwaves, etc.

Staging the Bathroom

The key to bathroom staging is arranging accessories in an open and soothing manner to highlight any details.

1. Arranging or rolling towels in decorative baskets

2. Towels tied with ribbons or decorative pins

3. Scented soap arrangements

4. Creams and hand lotions

5. Fancy moisturizing & facial jars

6. Decorative Body Scrubs

7. Display a couple of expensive looking bottles of perfumes or bubble bath.

Staging the Backyard

Use plenty of plants and potted flowers. If there is a table in your backyard, make it the focal point. Find or create an attractive center piece. Then, surround it with a special arrangement of colorful plating, silverware, plastic glasses and accenting napkins.

Furnishings

Be careful not to initially overspend on furnishings. Completing rooms can be expensive. Cutting your expenses until you get rolling is essential due to initially having to put dollars into advertising. So, in the process of converting your home to a vacation rental property, shop wisely. Hunt discount stores, garage sales, thrift stores and websites that feature used furniture. This may include friends who have items they no longer need or want.

Make sure the home is safe and the furnishings are positioned in a way that allows movement with ease. Be conscious of positioning furnishings, accessories, and freestanding objects in a way that does not create a hazard, especially considering children. Many accidents frequently occur in the home.

Many of us have heard the term "feng shui."

The Chinese art or practice of creating harmonious surroundings that enhance the balance of yin and yang, as in arranging furniture or determining the siting of a house (Random House Dictionary).

Well, have you ever gone into someone's home and you just couldn't put your finger on it? But, something didn't feel right? It could have been a number of things. Maybe it was the positioning of the furnishings. Maybe it was the color of the walls. Maybe it was the flooring, or even the lighting. Whatever it was, there was energy in the home or building that turned you off. You never felt fully comfortable during your visit.

Without claiming to be an expert on Feng Shui, the same

principle applies. Just like creating the right mood, you must also focus on creating the right energy in your home. Your home has to have an energy and a set-up that feel rights and comfortable for your guests.

Once again, reflecting on your most memorable vacation experiences will enable you to view your home from the perspective of your potential guests. But, you first must develop an attitude that every detail counts. You must see the significance of leaving nothing to chance and focusing on the small things as well as the large things. This includes making sure that all furniture and appliances are clean and in useable condition.

The best way to ensure that the equipment in your rental is in order is to develop an inspection checklist. This will remind you before each reservation what needs to be attended to before the next guest arrives. The checklist will keep you on point.

Don't try to wing it. This will only open the door to errors, mistakes and poor customer service. In the beginning you can easily remember many details. But, as the business grows and you gradually increase your number of bookings, it will become increasingly difficult to keep up with repairs. As long as you exercise discipline in completing this checklist before each check-in and after each check-out, then you'll be able to stay on top of things.

Sample Rental Inventory Inspection Checklist

Item	Inspected at Check-In	Inspected at Check-Out
Appliances		
Furniture		
Beds		
Electronics		
Comments		

a. All appliances must be in working order and clean.

b. All towels must be clean and neatly folded in the storage area. It's impressive to have them color collated.

c. Glassware, dinnerware and utensils should be presented

in a clean, neat and visually appealing manner. They should be free from spots, fingerprints, smears or layers of dust. People like to see their reflection on glassware and dinnerware. Also, make sure any hazardous utensils are stored in a hazard free area not easily accessible to children. Be particularly conscious of items with edges, especially knives or appliances with blades, such as a blender.

Focusing on simple changes and new twists with existing furnishings in your home is a critical part of the process in physically setting up your home. It can help you save lots of money and time. At the same time, you can't compromise quality. You want to maintain a mindset of giving renters the extras that make your home stand out from the rest. Because, if your set-up is more than satisfactory and your extras are apparent, this says to your guests that you value their business. Your effort in giving something more than usual to your guests, to ensure that they have a positive vacation experience, will pay off big time in future bookings and recidivism.

Now that we've discussed all the major components for legally setting up your business and physically setting up your home, we will move on to Step #3 which is "Effectively Market Your Home." But, on a final note, we'd like to provide some additional tips to assist you in physically setting up your home.

Additional Tips for Proper Set-Up

1. Make sure your property has all the things that vacationers want.

    a) Bedrooms with all the necessary furnishings including a bed, dresser, end tables, lamps, a television, and a closet for clothing storage.

    b) Kitchen with common appliances, cookware and utensils (refer to preferred items list in the Toolbox).

    c) Family room with a selection of dvd's, cd's, video games and board games.

    d) Bathrooms with plenty of towels, wash cloths, soap and toiletries.

    e) Decorative accessories are great but need to be placed in safe areas of the home that do not create a hazard.

    f) The removal of your personal pictures, personal artifacts, valuables, and any other personal items. It's a good idea to have a locked and restricted area where you can temporarily store your personal belongings until you regain occupancy of your home.

g) Sheets are a significant part of your homes inventory. Most vacationers probably purchase sheets themselves and know the difference between high quality and low quality brands. So, play it safe. Only purchase wrinkle-proof 300 and above thread count sheets.

h) Shop wisely for sheets. Make sure you have a large selection. Some of these sets already include the sheets that coordinate with the set. This will also make the process of decorating the bed much easier.

2. Showcase soft and vibrant lighting to establish the room's mood.

3. Display and arrange furniture and accessories in 1, 3 or 5 groupings.

4. Utilize soft fabrics such as silks, satins, cotton, wool and faux furs.

5. Purchase window dressings with clean simple lines.

6. Add creative objects and accessories to shelving, fireplace mantels, bookshelves and ledges to pre-determined areas.

Accessories that are commonly used to stage rooms:

a) plants

b) silk flowers

c) pillows

d) throw rugs

e) love seats

f) ottomans

g) mirrors

h) baskets

i) afghans

j) various size beds

EFFECTIVELY MARKET YOUR HOME

EFFECTIVE Marketing is a critical element to your success. You may have a great location and a great home with all of the amenities a vacationer could ever dream of. But, without the right marketing strategy, your property will be underexposed and you will not be able to command top dollar for your bookings.

Marketing success begins with a solid marketing strategy and a clear understanding of the unique features of your property that will be most appealing to prospective guests. It, however, is equally important that you begin to see yourself as a salesperson. This is significant because many individuals entering the business of vacation home rental have limited sales experience. Now that you've fully set-up your business, your focus needs to shift to sales and generating revenue to sustain the business. So, if you're going to start making money in the least amount of time possible, you must become comfortable being your own pitch person. Potential guests respond to the enthusiasm you project about your home and the positive vacation experience you are selling.

The information in this chapter offers great marketing tools that will expose your property to the world and allow you to successfully become your businesses publicist and manager. There are different avenues, approaches and strategies that you can utilize to market your vacation home rental. This ranges from networking and email blasts to social media and video streaming (regular promotions). Throughout this chapter, we'll discuss each of these methods and strategies. But, more importantly, we'll attempt to inspire your entrepreneurial spirit. Because, the greater your desire for financial freedom, the greater the reward you'll eventually gain.

Pricing

The nightly, weekly and monthly rate of your rental can be determined by a number of factors.

1. Supply and demand.
2. The season of the year.
3. Your competition.
4. The effectiveness of your marketing.

Determining the right price point requires research of the market as well as your gut instinct. Visit various vacation websites to compare rates in your neighborhood, city and state. Record the comparable and varying amenities and features that are offered. Then, weigh the potential impact of pricing too high or pricing too low on your ability to book your vacation rental property.

You can elect to modify your pricing at any time. But, vacation home rental rates commonly change seasonally just like hotels do. Assess your areas travel demand and times of the year when you can best capitalize. Peak season or high season is when travelers frequent your area the most. The low season or off peak season is the time to indicate discounts and additional promotions. Last minute deals and other eye catching values will also draw in travelers even if only out of curiosity.

Minimum Stays

The pay your mortgage in a weekend formula requires a 3 night minimum. It's to your advantage to advertise a minimum stay of 3 nights. Daily rentals require a higher frequency of checking in and checking out. This can become a very stressful task and not as cost effective.

Example of a Seasonal Pricing

Season	Start	End	Nightly	Weekly	Monthly
Spring	Mar 1	May 24	$550	$2,700	$7,500
Summer	May 25	Sept 10	n/a	$3,000	$8,000
Fall	Sept 11	Oct 31	$575	$2,850	$8,500
Winter	Nov 1	Mar 1	$600	$3,250	$8,000

*Sales tax and Cleaning fees are not factored in rental rates

Official Website

The worldwide web is an invaluable resource that most business owners underutilize. This is because most business owners are yet to fully fathom that every corner of the world is right at their fingertips. The internet is a vast, interconnected universe of people, businesses and instantly accessible information.

Just take a moment to think about the name. We're so used to hearing the abbreviation "www" that few of us take time to fully process or think about what "www" stands for. Well, "www" stands for "World Wide Web." I truly began to grasp the power of the internet when I fortuitously began reading *Crush It* by Gary Vaynerchuk. He shared his personal life experiences in using the internet to exponentially grow his family's wine business. Through social media and video streaming he used the internet to reach a clearly defined target market.

Immediately after reading *Crush It*, I immediately began to focus more of my time and energy on applying some of the same principles and strategies to grow my business through internet marketing. Now, less than a year later, nearly 90% of my leads and bookings are generated through the internet.

The internet provides you with the capability to communicate and get the message out about your service to anyone, anywhere in the world. This is why you should devote much of your time and energy to maximizing your internet marketing strategies. In doing so, you'll learn ways to work smarter and more efficiently in growing your business.

Now that you've been reminded of the power of the internet, it's time for you to create a website to promote your business. If you're not computer literate or tech savvy, there's no need to worry. There are a number of web hosting companies such as Webstarts and

Yahoo Site Builder that offer easy-to-follow web design software. You can register your domain name, start building your website and have your website up and running for less than $100. It will take you time to select a template design and begin creating web pages. But, by taking this extra time, you can save hundreds if not thousands of dollars instead of paying a website designer.

The visual appeal of your website is important. Your website is equivalent to a flashing billboard in Times Square. You have a message that you want to convey to prospective guests. And, the message you want to convey is that your home will provide them with a positive vacation experience. The hard part, however, is learning to convey your message to consumers in a way that will get them to buy into it.

Your website is more powerful than you can imagine. Even if you've never thought of it this way, you're building your brand in cyberspace. But, the content of your website needs to meet several conditions for it to be effective. One of those conditions is that your website has to hold the consumer's interest during the first few seconds of viewing your website. Images and content have to hit them in a way that triggers a positive emotional response compelling them to want to see more and learn more about your property.

The domain name that you choose is very important when advertising your image offline and online. It's the key to your businesses identity. Online customers must feel confident in your brands quality, promise and delivery. Unlike having a brick and mortar outlet of distribution, consumers are at a disadvantage having to trust what you're selling. Sure, they get a feel from the pictures and the descriptions in your ads. But, you must understand that they're still taking a chance on an unknown experience at your home. They're relying on your brand to deliver a positive vacation experience.

Information & Features to Highlight

1. **Logistics**

   The distance to and from major destinations is a key selling point of your property.

   Commonly asked questions:

   > How far is the property from the Airport?
   >
   > Where is the nearest grocery store?
   >
   > Where's the nearest rental car company?
   >
   > How far is the mall?
   >
   > Where's the nearest golf course?
   >
   > What type of family activities are nearby?
   >
   > What type of restaurants are nearby?
   >
   > How close are bars & nightclubs?

2. **Activities and Entertainment**

   The dining, arts and culture are world renowned in some tourist hot spots such as Las Vegas. But, some vacationers prefer to spend the majority of their vacation at the rental property. Therefore, you can appeal to these consumers by also highlighting the conveniences of home such as Wi-Fi, Video Games, Board Games, and DVD's.

3. **Number of Bedrooms**

   Primarily, vacationers need to know if your property can accommodate their needs.

4. **Floor Plan**

   Provide measurements and dimensions. Vacationers appreciate details about the layout of the home. The spaciousness of any room or of the entire property itself should be highlighted.

5. **Theme Rooms and Luxury Features**

   Vacationers are willing to pay for luxury features. So, if your property possesses any luxury features or added bonuses, you definitely want to emphasize them on your website.

   - Theatre Room
   - Exercise Room
   - Game Room (Poker Table)
   - Pool
   - Spa
   - Jacuzzi in the master bedroom
   - Furnishings & Décor
   - Fine Art
   - Sculptures

6. **Upgrades**
   - Gourmet Kitchen

- Appliances – stoves, subzero refrigerator, double oven
- Laundry Room - Front Loader

7. **Services**
   - Concierge Service
   - Butler Service
   - Personal Chef
   - Personal Trainer
   - Personal Shopper
   - Massage Therapist
   - Spa Treatment
   - Laundry/Cleaning Service
   - Childcare Service
   - Luxury Car Rental
   - Limousine Service
   - Private Jet Charters
   - Executive Security
   - Hair Stylist/Barber

Virtual Tours

Virtual tours are extremely important to building consumer confidence. This form of visual advertising reveals many of the intimate details of your home. And, it automatically answers many questions that potential guest may have. Given this, you must utilize all of the proper staging practices we previously discussed (in Step #2) to create the most impactful presentation.

First, you must decide if you'll produce the virtual tour yourself or hire a professional. Doing it yourself is the least expensive way to get it done. But, don't compromise quality. You must think of your home as being the star in a movie and yourself as the writer, director and producer.

A minimum of two to sixteen images should be captured in your virtual tour from the center of the scene. Below is a list of some of the basic equipment needed to film and produce your virtual tour. For a day shoot, equipment can be rented instead of purchased to save money.

Some of the basic equipment that will be needed:

- A quality digital or film camera
- A 90 degree panoramic tripod head
- Virtual tour software
- Lighting kit

Here are a few additional suggestions for creating an effective virtual tour:

- When shooting 360 degrees, proper lighting is always an issue.
- Utilize a balance of interior lighting and natural lighting to get the best shooting conditions.
- Sound effects and other functionalities can be added to your homes virtual tour.
- Touch-stitching software will allow you to process and retouch your stitched images.

Installing the virtual tour on the internet.

- Use Plug-in or Java script technology
- Java does not require a browser to play virtual tours.
- Plug-ins are available as free downloads on the web.

There are many options available for filming and producing your virtual tour. Your creative desire will dictate the direction you decide to take. Likewise, this decision will also be impacted by your budget. Another cost-effective strategy, if you can't afford to rent equipment for a day or hire a professional to film and produce your virtual tour, is to utilize Flash technology with the display of photos on your website.

Social Media

Social Media is a term that many people use loosely when referring to sites like Twitter, Facebook and LinkedIn. But, for individuals and companies who take the art and science of social media seriously, millions if not billions of dollars can be generated. Gail Z. Martin in her book *30 Days to Social Media Success* states that "social media is just a new vehicle for the old form of news: word of mouth." And, the new vehicle is the internet. So, you could be losing tons of money and working that much harder all because you're not continuously incorporating social media marketing into your marketing plan.

The goal is to become a lead generation machine. And, to

accomplish this in the most cost-effective and efficient manner possible, you must fully utilize the power of the internet. You must make a total commitment to studying and implementing every strategy possible to draw traffic to your website.

One way to accomplish this is by having individuals type in your company's website for a direct connection to your URL. The other way is to affiliate yourself with other related websites that already generate traffic to many of your targeted prospects. Individuals, then, can link to your company's website through affiliates.

Social media and portal websites are so powerful that these are the primary marketing strategies that I utilize to generate leads and to more importantly get bookings. Because the results have been so effective, I'm concentrating even more of my time and energy on mastering the art of social media. On a daily basis, I'm searching for new websites to form partnerships with and to gain their permission to create a reciprocal link.

Portal Websites

Portal sites target the vacation market but they also feature your competitors. The advantage of advertising your own website rather than participating in a portal website is that your website has no competition. Getting your official website optimized will drive traffic directly to you. And, if you concentrate on delivering an ad that is unique and that sets you apart from the competition, then you'll find a winning formula for marketing success.

The greatest benefit of portal websites is that they can provide you with exposure to your target market. They also will assist you with increasing the prominence and visibility of your company's website. Portal websites, in other words, can do the heavy lifting marketing work for you. But, you have to know how to utilize them effectively to get the best results.

Most portal sites make it easy for you to create a link. Some simply require you to point and click on your features. Additionally, many of the "Preferred Websites" in the Toolbox (Step #6 "Utilize the Toolbox Resources") like www.702vacationrentals.com are free. And, even the paid portal websites periodically have promotions or special offers.

Frequently browse paid portal sites to sign up for "free" trial memberships. This may result in one or more bookings. This will allow you to test the waters to see if the site is working for you. The average ad on some of the more popular portal websites like www.vacationhomerental.com costs more than $200. So, if you get one booking during the trial membership, it will have been more than worth it.

I suggest purchasing the Premium package if you decide to purchase an ad on a portal website. This is because Premium packages will give your ad the best exposure and are more likely to place you on the first page. The properties on the first page receive the largest number of hits.

A feature ad would be the next best option. Expect to pay more for a featured ad than a premium ad, but it generally is worth it. Some sites advertise that their feature ad could net your company 50% more exposure.

Your inquiries that come through a portal site most likely will have the same format. It's great to utilize your smart phone to respond to leads. By having your email application on your smartphone linked to your email, it allows you to respond to prospects without delay. Prospects are frequently shocked to receive a return phone call from me within five minutes of them submitting their inquiry. This significantly increases your chances of booking prospects.

The inquiries that pop-up on the e-mail application of my phone usually look something like:

Vacation website Rental Inquiry Notification

Listing# 234472

Description: Centennial Hills, Las Vegas

Nevada, USA, Desert Charm Estate

Luxury Estate

Name: Joan Turner

Email: jslots@vegastoy.com

Tel: 702 567- 0007

Arrival date: 10/31/13

Departure date: 11/7/13

# of Nights: 8

in Party: 6

Comment: Hello, we are looking for a nice home to accommodate us during our annual family vacation. Could you send me the total cost including all fees?

I immediately responded to Ms. Turner's inquiry. I answered her questions and successfully booked the lead. I received payment through PayPal within one hour of my initial phone contact with Ms. Turner.

Before we move on, there is one final note about portal websites. It's very important to maintain an up-to-date Availability Calendar. When visitors enter your site, it will provide greater credibility. You want visitors to see that your property is in high demand.

Fraudulent Inquiry

Increased traffic to your company's website can also mean increased viruses, increased spam in your emails, and increased scam artists. It baffles me that individuals would actually take the time to create a fake, fraudulent inquiry. But, they do. And, many people have been caught off guard. So, don't take this lightly. Prepare yourself to immediately identify the warning signs.

Warning Signs of a Fraudulent Inquiry:

1. The information in the inquiry doesn't make sense.
2. The telephone number and other information submitted are inaccurate.
3. The e-mail is from a free service.
4. The name and phone number is from outside the US.

5. They usually have a long drawn out story of needing temporary housing and are more than willing to send a check in advance. They are so eager to book that they're willing to overpay and let you send the deducted overpayment back to them.

6. They're unwilling to utilize pay-pal, credit cards or an international bank wire transfer.

7. They only want to pay via cashier's check.

8. They want to pay in full far in advance and only by cashier's check.

Below is an example of a fraudulent inquiry:

Name: Joan Turner
E-mail: joanturner@yahoo.com
Tel: 1 702 567-0007
Arrival date: 30 Oct 2013
Departure date: 7 Oct 2013
# of Nights 8
in Party 6
Comment: Hello, I am looking for a home to rent. I am coming to the United States to take an internship at the University of Nevada. I will be moving in the next two months and my family will be coming around two weeks later. I want to secure the home as soon as I can. I am willing to make a full payment.

The above inquiry is screaming scam and has some of the warning signs of a fraudulent inquiry. The telephone number is from Nevada's 702 area code. But, the date of requested rental is written in a European format. There also is a long draw out story. At the same time, I've had many successful bookings from International Tourists. So, don't automatically assume that the inquiry is fraudulent because the lead is from another country.

If you feel that you have a fraudulent scam, my suggestion is that you don't reply. Because, once you reply, they have now successfully obtained your e-mail address and you'll probably receive more fraudulent inquiries. There are 5 suggestions on how to safeguard your business from being a victim of Fraudulent Inquiries.

1. Do not answer obvious fraudulent inquiries.
2. Do not send refunds for cancellations until a minimum of two weeks after the date a check clears.
3. Do not send money back for overpayment.
4. Add a conservative refund policy in your agreement.
5. Conduct due diligence on the company affiliated with the inquiry.

Search Engine Optimization

1. Choose the right key words (keyword optimization).
2. Optimize your web pages (submit key words/phrases to search engines).
3. Get inbound links to your webpage (external site factors).

Optimizing your official website on search engines will give more prominence and visibility to your web page. Keywords are search words that internet users type to conduct an inquiry. The right keywords are words that generally describe the purpose of your site.

Be certain that the keywords contain simple text. The description of your site's content can increase your ranking. When selecting keywords, it's also important to conduct research on comparable keywords and phrases. This includes noting how these keywords and key phrases visually appear in the Search Results. Over time, by inserting keywords and key phrases into search engines, you'll greatly increase your chances of bringing more targeted traffic to your website.

Below are some examples of key words and key phrases for my company Desert Charm Estate:

- Desert Charm Estate
- Las Vegas Home Rental
- Las Vegas Luxury Vacation Rental
- Las Vegas Luxury Home Rental
- Las Vegas Estate
- Las Vegas Vacation Estate
- Vegas Luxury Estate Rental
- Luxury Estate Rental
- Vegas Vacation Estate
- Vegas Luxury Mansion
- Las Vegas Mansion Retreat
- Estate Rentals
- Vacation Home Rental

Now that you've created your keywords and key phrases, submit them to search engines yourself. Visit www.thesearchenginelist.com for a complete list of search engines to submit your key words and phrases. Just to get you started, one example of a search engine is: http://www.google.com/analytics/.

Your strategy should be to link your website to the best directories and other sites with topics related to the purpose and target market of your website. The best search engines "crawl the web" like a spider searching for links to your site. These crawlers interpret a link as a vote. The more votes you have coming from other sites the higher your page will rank. This will allow your page to receive better positioning in the search results page. Your goal should be to get as close to the first search result page for as many keywords and key phrases as possible.

One of the key things that a vacation home rental website can do to increase traffic is to exchange links with reputable and quality sites. The sites should be compatible to your sites topic. Ask the webmaster for a link exchange. This will generate increased traffic towards your target market and will improve your ranking with search engines.

Creating a Great Ad

Continuously and effectively advertising your vacation home rental property is another critical component in your formula for success. Classified ads generate leads and tapping into this lead generating avenue is easy and cost effective. You first have to learn how to develop and implement a cost-effective ad campaign that gets immediate results. You, then, want to prepare and post your ad in the shortest amount of time possible. This is because time is money.

Every ad campaign is unique to the location and type of property. Features and amenities highlighted for a cabin rental aren't the same as features and amenities that would be highlighted for an ocean rental. Whether or not a property is seasonal is one distinguishing factor.

Writing your Ad (The Vision)

When taking on the task of writing your ad for your vacation rental, remember that you're trying to paint a picture of a positive vacation experience. In essence, that's what you're selling. Make sure your ad is clear and concise. Make the ad spark imagination and excitement. The right photos and visual images will add spice and flavor to your presentation. Many of the elements discussed in creating a powerful website can be applied to writing a compelling ad. There should be a strong correlation between your website and your ad. In fact, you want to use many of the keywords and phrases from your website in your ad.

Sample Ad

Desert Charm Estates luxury mansion is located in the most exciting city in America, Las Vegas Nevada. This 8 bedroom, 4 ½ bath estate features a theatre room, chef kitchen, exercise room, outdoor kitchen, formal dining room, 35ft. pool and a 12-seater spa. The dramatic entryways, vaulted ceilings and stunning views make this the property the jewel of the desert. Enjoy the privacy and spaciousness of this 6500 sq ft. retreat. The home has been furnished with the finest furnishings and upscale décor that rivals any five-star accommodations.

Desert Charm Estate is just a short distance to the fabulous Las Vegas Strip. The Estate provides you with convenient access to world-class restaurants, nightlife, shopping, casino's, world-class golf courses and entertainment.

This fabulous home has been enjoyed by many travelers including Celebrities and VIP's. It's truly the best kept secret. You, too, can enjoy the best at Desert Charm Estates.

Visit our official website for a list of services we offer such as a personal chef, spa treatment, limousines, exotic cars, VIP hosting and much more (www.desertcharmestate.com).

For Reservations call (702) 704 9099 or toll free 1 (855) 334-8433.

Proofreading Your Ad

Make sure your ad is grammatically correct. Typos and other errors can compromise the ad. Make sure the ad is effective in relaying all the facts. Get feedback from others before you post the ad.

Post Classified Ads

Posting information in classified ads and online classified ads is another free or low cost way of gaining visibility and increasing traffic to your website. There are a multitude of websites that enable you to post classified ads (see a preferred list in Step #6: The Toolbox). Finally, when creating and implementing an effective ad campaign using classified ads, it's important to post them a minimum of three times a week.

Networking

Social Media is a very powerful source for spreading the news about your vacation home rental business. But, there's something else that's nearly as powerful. And, it's called Networking.

Statistically the web accounts for a small percentage of all vacation rentals. This is according to a PhoCus Wright Analyst report which found that approximately two-thirds of vacation rental consumers conduct their research online. But, only 27% of vacation rental owners list their properties through an online vehicle (www.phocuswright.com). This means that as powerful as the internet is as a social medium it still has a long way to go.

Personal offline marketing still is the most popular and important form of advertising. The art of people connecting to other people because of common interests or to provide a product or service is a universal phenomenon. But, you must have a mindset to want to intentionally use this phenomenon to your advantage.

Creating a Fan Club is your first assignment in creating a formal structure for building your network. Through your Fan Club, you can send members email correspondence or mailings promoting your vacation rental property. But, more importantly you'll continuously be promoting excitement about your company and what your company has to offer - which is a positive vacation experience. And, as a result of your enthusiasm, others will automatically want to spread the word about what you have to offer.

Secondly, you want to set a goal of how many people you want to talk to a day about your vacation rental property. However, don't neglect other forms of social media and traditional forms of marketing such as distributing business cards and flyers.

People who can help you Build Your Network:

1. Family, Friends and Co-Workers are a good place to start your fan club.
2. Strangers (Outgoing, Talkative People).
3. People in the Rental Industry (Real Estate Agents, Property Managers, Travel Agents, Hotel Managers, Event Coordinators).
4. People in the Transportation Industry (Cab Drivers, Bus Drivers, Limousine Drivers, Airline Employees). They deal directly with travelers. And, travelers will respect their opinion.
5. Endorsements from Celebrities, Athletes and Entertainers (in addition to VIP Service companies).
6. Other Vacation Home Rental Owners (refer bookings to one another).

Referral & Affiliate Reward Programs are another way to get the word out. These programs require structure when setting them up. But, the incentive of paying people to spread the word about your company is an excellent one. Here are four suggestions in setting up a good referral program:

1. Create a package for prospective affiliates to read.
2. Give various incentives in the package to get them to join the program.
3. Keep it short and to the point. Quickly show them how they're going to benefit (no more than 5 pages).
4. Organize your file keeping system. Keep an accurate account of leads and commissions. Your payment history and paperwork will need to be cataloged and accessible for easy reference.

Don't over complicate your referral program. People really want to know how they can benefit from sending business your way. The bottom line "How can I get paid".

The best businesses to solicit for participation in your referral program are the ones that cater to the same target prospects. You can also check-out online affiliate marketing programs.

These are the five major things you must make clear when presenting your affiliate program to businesses:

1. The mission of your business.
2. How both businesses will benefit?
3. How the business owner gets paid?
4. What other incentives will the business owner receive for participating in the program?
5. How long will it take to get paid from the A&R program?

Payment

Preparing to collect payments is another important part of setting up your business. There are several ways to collect payment. The most common ways that vacation home owners collect payments are: PayPal, checks, money order, cashier's check and wire transfer. Cash is always an acceptable form of payment. In some local rental situations it may be used for deposits but mostly cash comes into play to clear up balances of payments and security deposits.

Adding a reservation management system link is another option. A payment page can be added to your vacation rental website by an independent company that will process the reservations for you. This could be used as an alternative if you don't have a merchant account. It also allows you to process automated payments online. Most portal sites have options to process credit card payments directly through their website and credit the payment to your account.

I strongly suggest getting a merchant account for your business. This will allow you to process your reservations by accepting major credit cards. The speed at which you can process a credit card payment will directly affect your ability to close the deal. So, set-up a payment system that makes the payment process as easy as possible for your prospects to finalize their plans and to avoid the potential negative impact of buyer's remorse.

Wire transfers and Cashier's checks are the least advantageous method of collecting funds due to many scams that are running rampant on the internet.

Collecting Security Deposits

Always collect a security deposit for possible damages. Though it's not full-proof, holding a security deposit is a big deterrent for excessive damages and items being removed from the home. When collecting security deposits, be mindful that people don't like their money being held for long periods of time. So, in your security deposit policy, have a reasonable time frame to return the money. It should usually happen once it's been confirmed that everything is in order.

Make sure that you deduct a reasonable and fair replacement or repair cost if something is damaged. Honest mistakes do happen. However, even better, I strongly recommend that you purchase an insurance policy against any damage to your property for each booking. Specialized Vacation Home Rental Damage Protection should be purchased from a reputable company like Travel Guard. Additionally, vacationers may also purchase a separate policy which will greatly assist your ability to book your rental. The purchasing of insurance by one or both parties can eliminate the amount of the security deposit being a deal breaker by alleviating having to collect a large security deposit from renters. This will automatically increase the likelihood of increasing your bookings.

Cancellation Policy

Every owner has the right to design a cancellation policy with which they feel comfortable. I personally prefer a cancellation policy that doesn't require me to return any money to guests. So, my policy is "No Refunds." And, my rental agreement clearly spells out this policy. And, I verbally review this with guests when signing the agreements and rental rules.

My critics may say this is a little unfair. I would then tell them that my business can't afford to be a victim of an indecisive vacationer. Unlike the hotels, I only own one vacation home Desert Charm Estates. So, if a prospective guest cancels, they just cost me business from another lead or prospect that I could have closed or pursued to secure a booking. Because things do happen, it's only fair to have a cancellation policy that considers emergencies. But, an owner does have the right to protect his or her interests. So, carefully consider drafting a cancellation policy that will protect you from losing financially while still being fair to the renters.

Make sure they sign off on all your policies indicating that they clearly understand the terms and conditions. Be clear about your policies with regards to exchange of the payment to avoid any misunderstandings.

Close the Deal

You've been empowered with many strategies and techniques to effectively market your vacation rental property. But, now that you've drawn the leads to you, it's important to know how to convert your leads into bookings. Without sales, there's no revenue being generated. Without revenue, there's no business.

Rule #1 Be Confident in your ability to sell.

In this business you will wear many hats but the most important one is that of a deal maker. You are your homes best sales person. You now have to use your real estate knowledge, sales person knowledge, photographer knowledge, travel agent knowledge and telemarketing skills. Most importantly, the ability for you to become a total stranger's friend is critical in order to close a deal. You have to do all of this while on the clock due to the fact they have a good selection of vacation homes to choose from but their interest was piqued by yours. Developing a good rapport with your client is a key to setting your home apart from the rest. This is a great strategy to show potential guests why they should choose your property.

Rule # 2 Listen to your client's needs.

An old supervisor once told me "Listen with two ears and one mouth." In other words, focus on finding out what are your customer's expectations. If you're able to meet them, then you'll probably close the deal.

Rule # 3 Gain your client's trust.

In my first year of sales, a supervisor gave me the best advice ever. He told me that if your presentation is strong, factual and you become your client's friend along with diligent follow-up, you strengthen the possibility of closing the deal. The key ingredient to sales is "Becoming Your Clients Friend."

People buy from people they like. It's just that simple. Therefore, the more contact you have with the vacationer, the more you enhance your chances of booking them at your property. You must be willing to do what advertising agencies do. They repeatedly follow-up. And, trust me. Advertising agencies wouldn't be in business if they didn't consistently follow-up with clients.

Simply by following-up in a timely manner, you will increase your chances of booking a client by 50% or more. But, it's important to make contact within the first 3 hours of the inquiry. That's when the bonding begins.

Most of your follow-up to leads generally is by e-mail, phone or a combination of the two. I suggest using both. People are more likely to close a deal with someone they talk to. This means that a lot of the times, the impression you make via telephone can make or break a deal. So, be prepared to use your telemarketing hat a lot. After establishing rapport, shift your focus to selling them on the property. Give them all the necessary information they need to decide whether or not to book the reservation.

In the middle of this process, you're looking for the right moment to pull the trigger and wrap up the deal. The more deals you close the better you'll become at recognizing the pivotal moment. Becoming a top closer is the goal. And, your job is to lead your vacationer down the road that leads to "Yes."

Top closers are able to bring the vacationer down the road to "Yes" in one phone call. It's a skill that most telemarketers are trained in to generate revenue for companies every day.

Rule #4 Show the value of what you're selling.

Your ability to demonstrate the value of your property vs. the value of another property can be the difference between closing and not closing the sale. Think about the last time you visited the car dealership and spoke to a salesperson. If he or she was a good salesperson, they didn't give you the price of the car you were interested in until they first attempted to build its value. They probably informed you of its gas mileage, customized paint job, horse power, upscale interior, sound system, chrome rims, racing tires etc. If he or she was an experienced salesperson, they didn't mention the price of the car until after they had successfully built up the value of the car. It makes the pricing seem fair, justified and in some cases a clear bargain.

Showing your home's value to your potential guest is one of the things that will determine whether or not vacationers chose to stay at your home. You can show value in many different ways:

- The money they save compared to what others offer.
- The location to nearby activities and events.
- Your homes set-up.
- Your homes features.
- Your homes environmental assets.
- The service of your homes staff and management.

Acting as the concierge for your guest will get you increased bookings. If your rapport is great and you show the value of your home, you've now succeeded in being the go to person for your guest's vacation. They will use you in that capacity. So, be prepared. All of these value points will create a demand for your vacation package. When it's done properly, it'll be very difficult for your competition to match your sales presentation. However, you should always be prepared for rebuttals. The words "I don't know" should never be in your vocabulary. Instead replace them with "I will get that information for you shortly."

Answering questions come with the business, but if you are prepared with the right answers these exchanges make you come across as a knowledgeable and helpful expert. On the other hand, giving too much information without the intention or the ability to properly close is becoming a tourist help desk. And, that's not what you want. So, it's very important to find a balance between disclosing the right amount of information. Ultimately, success is measured by closing the deal. So, build your confidence and ability to sell the value of your property by practicing with a script.

Rule #5 The sale is never dead.

I was amazed in my first year of sales that some of my co-workers and counterparts were so quick to say that a sale was dead. To the contrary, I've always strongly believed that a sale is never dead. My attitude has always been that if a customer doesn't buy today, there's always tomorrow. Being successful in any sales-driven business requires a willingness to do what the next person is not willing to do. And, part of that is being persistent without being a pest. It's a belief that you will eventually win your client's respect and earn their trust to make the purchase. During the process, you must use your best qualities to persuade and convey all of what your vacation home has to offer. This is the art of sales. It's understanding that people have to feel that having you as their salesperson is just as valuable as what they are purchasing.

Your salesmanship also is a key to establishing a fan base. All the clients whose interest is piqued but don't select your home to rent for their vacation will become part of your database. Thus, they can be marketed to in the future. And, at any given moment, they may change their mind and decide to book some dates. On numerous occasions, I've received a call from a prospect that previously was ambivalent. Then, one day, sometimes months later, they call with their credit card in hand eager to book my vacation rental.

Summary

The possibilities for the growth of your business are endless once you learn how to effectively market and become a strong salesperson. Effective marketing requires discipline, patience and persistence. And, not to be underestimated, a clearly written marketing plan is essential because it increases the chances of focused follow-through. Effective marketing also requires a clear understanding of the power of social media and networking. With this understanding, you'll always strive to maximize your reach through building your online and offline network.

The information in this chapter provides an overview of marketing tools and strategies that can be implemented to increase the exposure of your property to the world. From search engine optimization to the art of closing deals, there is much to learn if you want to generate sustainable revenue for your business. Once leads start pouring in from your marketing efforts and deals are being closed, you'll then have to learn how to manage a fully operational business. And, having read this far, I'm confident that you're up to the challenge.

MANAGE YOUR VACATION HOME RENTAL

PHYSICAL maintenance of your property is one aspect of "Managing Your Business." Administrative tasks and duties is another aspect. Thus, it's important that you put a system in place as soon as possible to closely monitor and attend to both aspects of your business.

Your vacation rental property must be well maintained if you're going to have a highly successful business. It is critical that you take pride in your residence and exercise a certain degree of discipline in following through with the necessary upkeep. On numerous occasions, vacation home rental businesses have suffered greatly because of "bad" online reviews. And, in many of these instances, the poor reviews were avoidable. They primarily were the result of many owners' failure to consistently pay attention to detail.

Your ultimate goal should be to maintain a 99% occupancy rate. This is relative to the number of days per month you and your family may or may not want to make your space available to vacationers. But, to accomplish such a lofty goal, you must have an awareness of the various factors that contribute to a formula for success. Then, you must accept full responsibility for following through with the clear business management plan and marketing strategies that have been clearly outlined for you in the *Freedom Guide*.

Seven General Priorities for Effectively Managing Your Business

1. **Reservations**: Keeping detailed reservation information and an accurate record of incoming and outgoing guests is critical. Create an individual file for each guest with all of their information and paperwork. File them in a location that is easily accessible for immediate retrieval.

2. **Updating your properties availability** calendar weekly is also very important. A reservation calendar will help keep you organized as well as fully informing potential guests about current vacancies. Potential Vacationers like to see dates that other vacationers have previously reserved. This sends a message that your property is in demand. The vacationer in turn may be more prone to secure their date due to the demand in fear that someone else may book their desired dates. This along with good reviews adds to the credibility of your property.

3. **Screening Guest**: It begins with the initial contact. Focus on gathering information pertaining to the purpose of

your guests visit. Determine if it's a regular vacation, a special occasion, business travel, or a spur of the moment event. Then, review and verify their information for accuracy. You should obtain a copy of the primary renters' driver's license or state ID along with their home and work information. A background check is costly and intrusive. But, it can send a message to guests that they must adhere with property rules and possibly lessen the likelihood of major incidents occurring. Losing a large deposit and the threat of legal recourse can be a big deterrent for most individuals, even those who frequently bend or break rules. Don't be afraid of being nosey. After all, this is your property and you're the owner of the business. The liability falls on you. So, you must protect your interest.

4. **Check-in & Check-out Procedures**: It's very important that someone checks guest in and checks them out. I call this person the Guest Coordinator. Check-in is essential to setting the tone and laying down the ground rules. It also gives you an opportunity to meet your guests in person to formally greet them and to observe their interaction with other guests in their party.

5. **House Rules**: Develop a clear, concise, well written list of House Rules to be presented to guests prior to and during Check-In. Your Policies & Procedures and House Rules provide guests with clear guidelines regarding their

conduct during their stay at your property. Below are some of the common behaviors you want to address in your house rules:

a. Leaving lights and other appliances on.

b. Moving furnishings.

c. Leaving trash and garbage in the home.

d. Leaving doors unlocked.

e. Leaving personal items behind after Check-out.

f. Unauthorized parties or large events on the property.

g. Leaving rooms in disarray.

h. Parking in undesignated areas.

i. Unauthorized services utilized or performed on the property.

Verbally reiterate the fire safety instructions during the walk thru. Physically show guests all fire exits.

a. Show guests the location of fire extinguishers. Have them accessible for guest in case of a fire. At least one fire extinguisher should be located on each floor and near the kitchen.

b. If your home has two stories, make sure that there are portable ladders (roll downs) that are easily accessible. Show guests where they're located and demonstrate proper usage.

c. Inspect all of your smoke detectors and carbon dioxide detectors.

d. Ensure that the floor plan and Fire Safety Policy are visible throughout the house.

Post an Emergency Contact and Reference list in a visible location. The entryway or kitchen is an ideal location for posting. The list should include:

    a.   The owner or managements contact info.

    b.   The location to the nearest hospital.

    c.   Handyman's number.

    d.   Police & fire info.

    e.   Pharmacy information.

Vendors that are affiliated with your business should be available for 24 hour service. Getting someone out to your home to fix a leak or an electrical problem in a timely manner is a high priority. You never want to inconvenience or disrupt your guest's vacation experience. Some issues may be beyond the handyman's ability to immediately repair. But, the most important thing is to clearly and honestly communicate with your guests to provide them with updates and to reassure them that you are doing everything within your power to resolve the problem in a timely manner.

Guests also need to be reminded of the consequences of infractions and non-compliance with house rules. Obtain their signature and issue them a copy.

6. **Correspondence with Guests**: Speaking directly with guests will significantly reduce the likelihood of miscommunication. Regular communication through phone calls, emails and text messages allows both parties to remain fully informed of every detail related to your

guests scheduled stay at your property. E-mailing and texting are two of the most popular ways of reaching out to guests and to ensure a quick response. However, you shouldn't abandon the traditional method of mailing letters to your guests. Traditional mail has a personal touch, especially if it's hand written or typed with an original signature. Thus, personalized letters and instructions mailed to guests demonstrate that you're willing to take extra time on their behalf.

Welcome Package: The Guest Welcome Package greets guests and provides a wealth of information. When creating your welcome package be certain to highlight all of the important information and policies. Be creative. At minimum, a good welcoming package should include:

- A welcome letter
- The house rules
- The policies and procedures
- Going Green Policy
- Emergency contact information
- Brochures and information for activities and services

Exit Letter: This letter can be given at check-out or mailed to guests after their departure. Sending your guests a letter to let them know that you appreciated their stay adds another personal touch. Satisfied guests share their excitement about their vacation experience with friends, family, and associates. And, they are prime targets for joining your fan club.

7. **Payment**: Receiving the initial rental deposit is confirmation that you have a deal. Never allow your guest to wait to pay when they arrive. They easily may cancel their reservation without you receiving any form of compensation. Collect your deposit or full payment in advance. At minimum, collect a reservation deposit. I would strongly suggest obtaining your payment in full depending on the total amount of the agreement. Fifty percent is adequate if the agreement is a large amount. My rule of thumb is that any stay of 3 days or longer requires a 50% deposit.

Stipulate your payment policy in your agreement so there won't be any misunderstandings. Also strive to provide your guest with payment options that are easy and convenient. PayPal is a great way to take payments quickly and safely particularly if you and the client have never met in person. Other acceptable forms of payment are major credit cards, money orders and checks.

Paperwork

Paperwork that is well organized and covers all important aspects of your business is essential. There are a number of standard documents you will need such as: Agreements, House Rules, Check-In & Check-Out Procedures, Receipts, and Attestation Forms. We've provided you with a number of sample forms in the "Toolbox (Step #6)."

You will also need forms for any services that you may offer. An example of this is providing grocery shopping services to your guests. At minimum, you want to create a form so that you can provide a record of service to the guest, for your general filing and to assist you with bookkeeping.

It's also important to customize your paperwork. Every property is not the same. A cabin retreat and a SoHo flat may have some similarities in terms of offering a positive vacation experience. But, because of their different physical locations, there inherently are different liabilities. You, therefore, need to create different forms to address the unique elements of your particular property. Primarily, you want to assess any potential liabilities because unforeseen issues will arise. And, you want to be as prepared as possible to avoid or prevent any potential emergencies.

Security of the Home

I doubt that you need to be reminded of the importance of security. Just as your home is an asset you want to protect, so are your guests. And, just as you go the extra mile to make your guests feel comfortable, you also want to reassure them that they are safe.

Changing locks after every visit can be costly. Thus, you want to find an inexpensive way to safeguard your home without tons of keys to your property floating around. I suggest placing more than one lock on the front door. This provides vacationers with access by using one lock. Then, once they check-out, you can use the other lock without being immediately concerned with replacing the lock.

Another cost-saving strategy is to purchase a lock that has codes. The combination to the lock can simply be changed for each party. If you're not handy, it's also best to find a locksmith that you trust and are comfortable with to build a long-term relationship.

The check-in time of guests frequently varies. When the owner is unable to meet guests at their scheduled check-in time, your guests will need to check themselves into the property. A lock combination box is the best way to accommodate this. This key is securely stored while providing guest with immediate access.

Burglar Alarm

Burglar Alarms provides an additional layer of security and peace of mind. This applies to theft and fire. Your alarm system can be programmed to alert the security company, fire department and police department in the event of an emergency. By having a burglar alarm system, potential intruders are forewarned of your heightened security.

Purchasing a burglar alarm system that is equipped with a cell back up is vital. This feature will notify you via cell phone if your home has been compromised by an intruder. Most burglar alarm systems operate based on a land-line system. But, a cell back-up will enable your burglar alarm system to continue working in the event of a power outage or if you phone line is intentionally cut.

Video Surveillance

CCTV capability and a quality DVR are features you should

seek when purchasing a video surveillance system. Day/Night cameras can be positioned around the perimeter of your home such that every camera angle to your home can be viewed from a remote location. This will enable you to monitor the activity of your visitors, via computer or smart phone, when you are not on the premises. This includes watching guests check-in and check-out as well as recording license plate numbers.

Trust a neighbor

Most of us have a pretty good relationship with one or more of our neighbors. If not, it's important that you develop some kind of rapport with at least one of your neighbors. At some point in time, you'll need their assistance in giving you feedback on the activities of guests. A common example of this is when renters exceed the number of contractually permitted guests on the premises; or, when music is being played too loudly during parties.

Flood Lights

Flood lights increase your properties visibility. Because of this, they automatically serve as an additional deterrent to potential intruders. This is even more significant when the owner doesn't reside at the rental property. Your extended absences from the property are more likely to go unnoticed.

Excellent Customer Service
(Go the Extra Mile)

The bestselling book *Raving Fans* by Ken Blanchard teaches organizations and sales people from all industries how to understand what customers really want and how to use that to their advantage. In his book, he shares a story about a Mr. Farley a department store owner. Other employees couldn't understand how Mr. Farley ever got any work done because he spent so much time engaged in dialogue with his customers. In fact, many customers went out of their way to say "Hi" to Mr. Farley every time they visited the department store.

The wisdom of Mr. Farley was that he saw customer service as his most important job and number one priority. So, he worked just as hard at providing excellent customer service as he did in offering great discounts and keeping a fully stocked inventory. Once you develop a mindset and a strategic system of delivering extraordinary customer service, you will experience the same positive results as Mr. Farley. Your vacation home rental business fans will turn into spending fans.

Raving fans are the wheels to your lead machine. Highly satisfied customers eagerly make referrals. But, you must first believe in the power of customer service if you're going to maximize your sales. Many individuals are able to get bookings. But, how do you increase the rate of your guests returning to your property year after year? The answer is excellent customer service.

Understanding the entire sales process is also a key to being successful. There is lead generation and then there is fulfilling the obligation of what was advertised to your customers. In other words, you can't false advertise because customers will call you on it. And, one untimely lapse in providing customer service can be the downfall of your business.

The Ryan Beck Effect

The Ryan Beck Effect is another wonderful illustration of the power of customer service. On my very first sales job, and in my very first team meeting, my supervisor shared a very inspiring story with the team. The story was about a tailor name Mr. Ryan Beck who had been in business for over 50 years. His shop was located on Madison Avenue in Midtown Manhattan. My supervisor was elated to tell us the story of what he thought was the secret to Mr. Beck's longevity and success in business. I later learned that Mr. Beck actually was my supervisor's tailor. He made all of his custom suits which were priced at more than $1,000 each. But, based on the strength of referrals from business associates, my supervisor felt that it would be more than worth the investment.

Mr. Beck only saw his clients by appointment. My supervisor's first appointment with Mr. Beck was at 3pm January 2, 2001. My supervisor vividly recalled meeting Mr. Beck for the first time and was immediately impressed by his professionalism and attention to detail. After his fitting, my supervisor was asked to fill out Mr. Beck's questionnaire. It was a simple form that asked for the usual information such as name, address, telephone number, date of birth, religion, and occupation. No e-mail address was requested. Mr. Beck was from the old school and didn't use a computer.

Three weeks later, my supervisor returned to the shop to pick up his suit. He was picking up his suit in time for a romantic dinner with his fiancé celebrating his birthday. On the way out the door, Mr. Beck handed him an envelope and told him to enjoy his birthday. Still in shock from Mr. Beck's words, my supervisor opened up the card on the way home and it read "Enjoy your special day. Your next visit is 10% off."

My supervisor really appreciated the fact that Mr. Beck took the time to give him a card especially when he never mentioned anything about his birthday. But, the story gets better. Feb 2, 2001 at approximately 3pm, my supervisor received a phone call from Mr. Beck. He stated he just wanted to know how he liked the suit and how his family was doing. He also wanted to know if he would like to set-up an appointment for any additional services.

Then, March 2, 2001 at approximately 3pm, my supervisor received another call from Mr. Beck informing him of some great new fabrics that just came in. He asked my supervisor if he'd like to set-up an appointment.

The pattern continued. Mr. Beck called him every month on the second day of each month at approximately the same time. Like clockwork, he would also send a birthday card, holiday card, or discount cards. Mr. Beck would also hand him gifts for special occasions at his appointments. Eventually, my supervisor anticipated receiving a phone call from Mr. Beck to schedule his next appointment.

Mr. Beck was a simple man. He had one assistant and one location. Yet, without any additional advertising outside of personal mailings and business cards, he was one of the most sought after tailors in Manhattan. This is because he developed a system that delivered a high quality product along with impeccable customer service. He was willing to do the extra little things that his competitors weren't willing to do.

I've tried to emulate Mr. Beck's practices in my professional sales career and in my vacation home rental business. I call it the "Ryan Beck Effect." What I took away from the story was that Mr. Beck's friendliness, thoughtfulness, and meticulous attention to things that others in his industry would not take the time to do put him far beyond his competitors in the minds of his customers. He also made a lot of friends & fans along the way.

5 Keys to Producing "The Ryan Beck Effect"

1. Quality product & service.
2. Organized and precise follow-up.
3. Attention to detail.
4. Keeping things simple.
5. Doing personal things for your clients that your competitors don't do.

Continuous Advertising

Continuously and effectively advertising your vacation home rental property is another critical component in your formula for success. Classified ads generate leads and tapping into this lead generating avenue is easy and cost effective. In creating an effective ad campaign using classified ads, the key is to post them multiple times.

However, you first have to learn how to develop and implement a cost-effective ad campaign that gets immediate results. And, you want to create your ad in the shortest amount of time possible. Time is money.

Every ad campaign is unique to the location and type of property. Features and amenities that would be highlighted for a cabin rental would not be the same as features and amenities highlighted for an ocean rental. One distinguishing factor is whether or not your rental is seasonal.

Internet marketing is a key element to the success of your business. So, if you don't have a computer, I strongly suggest you purchase one, borrow one, or locate the closest library that offers access to the internet. Once you've taken pictures with your digital camera, you need access to a computer to download them and to store them in your archive.

Promotions

Online coupons are an easy advertising strategy to continuously implement. You can offer discounts for holidays, special occasions like birthdays or even for referring someone to your property.

Vacation Affirmations

Club Med has some of the best ads for vacations. To this day, ever since I was about ten years old, I remember one of their ads promoting their vacation club membership. I think the jingle went something like "Club Medification, the antidote for civilization." I remember how relaxing the ad made me feel and the visual images that were stimulated by the ad. I felt the ocean breeze as I laid on the beach with sand between my toes. The ad and the emotions the ad invoked in me is what I call a Vacation Affirmation.

I send letters and emails to my Fan-Club on a regular basis to try to invoke the same emotion. Sending text messages with Vacation Affirmations is another great strategy to peak interest. But, you must be consistent and send them out on a regular basis. You also want to post them to Social Media Sites. You'll be surprised by the response. Friday afternoons near the end of the workday, and possibly after a demanding work week, is a perfect time. Just imagine yourself receiving an email or text message that reads:

"Mr. Johnson it's time for some Rest and Relaxation (R&R). Desert Charm Estates Vacation Rental is ready and available to help you de-stress. Call now to Reserve!!!! Toll Free at (855) 334-8433 or visit www.desertcharmestate.com.

Instant Messages

Sending Instant Messages/Text Messaging sometimes catches prospective renters at a time when they were thinking about planning a vacation or a quick weekend getaway. Something like "It really is time for some R&R" could spark their interest. Your consumer might decide to take a look at your link or give you a call to further inquire about your offer.

Advertising Testimonials

Testimonials are another way to increase your bookings. People want to know what other people have to say about their vacation experience at your property. Testimonials including vacationers experience and opinion of your home are heavily considered by travelers looking for vacation home accommodations. Their interpretation and description of the things they liked about your home and your service leave an impression. And, that first impression is whether or not you provide excellent customer service and if your property is well maintained.

Don't rest on the great testimonials you received from highly satisfied customers. It only takes one negative testimonial to bring down London Bridge. Strive for perfection. Learn from each mistake and do your best to resolve problems as quickly as possible. When building a business you don't need any unexpected setbacks. Always stay focused on providing a great vacation experience to your clients.

People respect other vacationer's experiences and you want all the feedback on your clients experience to be great. The Fan-Club testimonials are a powerful marketing tool, and it's free. Testimonials on Blogs and other website sources will give you a clear advantage over the competition. Be proud of yourself and spread the good news. If no one knows what a great job you're doing, you won't receive the benefits. But, once you consistently start spreading the news, it adds up to money in the bank. So, take the extra time to use good reviews as an advertising and marketing tool.

Contests

I recently decided to advertise a contest on my official website. Participants were invited to "Register to win a 7 day New Year's Vacation!" It was a great way to obtain the contact information of several hundred registrants. My fan club has since doubled in size. Contests also are a great way to increase exposure and traffic to your website.

Giveaways

Branded items such as t-shirts, coffee mugs, and key chains are great promotional items. You can even add slogans like "I love to stay at my summer home." These items can be included in your guests Welcome Package or given away as part of contests. A pen with your homes title and phone number is a common giveaway among many companies particularly within the hotel industry. So, you don't have to fully reinvent the wheel. Just focus on the goal which is to keep your company's brand on the mind of consumers and to gain repeat business.

Referral Programs

Momentum is stirred by referrals and positive word of mouth. As you build relationships with your guests, you will find that they are the best source for your business growth. Business owner A tells business owner B what a great time they had at your home. And, the next thing you know, your phone rings with a new booking.

As the captain of this ship, you must take the helm. Part of your duty in navigating the ship is to design an effective Referral Program that keeps your well-oiled machine moving. You should give rewards and discounts to those who participate in your Referral Program. Let your Fan Club share a piece of the pie. Rewarding your clients for spreading the word is good business.

Discounts, cash credits, and complimentary days are just some of the incentives that can be included in the design of your reward program. Once again, you must be consistent in communicating with members of your Fan Club through emails to provide them with updates on your Reward Program. It makes them feel special and that you haven't forgotten about them.

Newsletters & Articles

Creating a newsletter keeps your fan club up-to-date on information regarding your property. Sending them info on attractions, sporting events, upcoming events will create travel interest. You can also inform them of deals and specials.

Writing articles is excellent P.R. Travelers love to read stories about other vacationer's experience. It also is an opportunity to provide more in-depth information on a particular subject matter as well as to highlight features and amenities of your property.

Last-Minute Deals

Vacationers are very fickle. If the deal is right, a person who wasn't planning a vacation can suddenly book based on impulse. Last-minute deals fill open dates and provide opportunities for discounts. Some vacationers don't like to get caught up in planning. They, instead, love being spontaneous in their decision-making, and you can capitalize on their impulsive spending habits. You can target some of your advertising efforts to these types of individuals by posting ads on websites that specifically advertise last-minute deals.

Coupons

Circulating coupons for your vacation rental can significantly increase your business. But, you have to learn the right way to use them as a marketing tool. Because coupons have been around for decades, people often take them for granted and they can go unnoticed. But, you can capitalize on the fact that people like to redeem coupons for discounts and savings, especially in a tough economy. Remember that what you're really saying to consumers is that they're getting a bigger value for their money.

There are several methods and strategies you can use to circulate your coupons. I suggest you begin by including them in your e-mails, particularly in your monthly or quarterly newsletter. Coupons with designated expiration dates can upturn your business during lull periods. There are a number of websites that will advertise your coupons for you for free or for a small fee.

Incentives

The incentives you offer vacationers, sometimes, make a difference between a guest deciding to stay at your property or another property in the same area. Free items and specials stimulate excitement and a feeling that you're willing to work hard to earn your guest's business. And, as an owner, you can still run a profitable business by offering incentives like complimentary days for extended stays and complimentary housekeeping every three days.

Summary

You now have a better understanding of how important it is to maintain a sense of organization with your paperwork and with your marketing strategies. Otherwise, instead of swimming, your business will quickly sink. Even though there are many hats that you must wear as an owner, managing the business of a vacation home rental can be enjoyable, fun and profitable when done correctly. Whenever you're feeling overwhelmed, simply review Step #4 along with the written plans that you have developed. You will quickly be reminded that you are more prepared to successfully navigate the challenges of vacation home rental ownership.

HOME MAINTENANCE

Maintenance

MAINTAINING the physical appearance of your property is one of the most important aspects of managing your vacation home rental business. You've already learned the importance of customer service in attracting vacationers and in gaining their repeat business. Maintenance, just like a branch is an extension of a tree, should be view as an extension of customer service. Therefore, maintenance should be your #1 priority.

Your ability to empathize with your guests, to put yourself in their shoes, is a valuable asset in maintaining the proper perspective on maintenance. No one wants to spend their vacation in a home that has poor maintenance. And, if the shoe were on the other foot, you'd probably do everything within your power to get management to immediately fix any repairs as well issue a discount or refund.

It's very unlikely that your business will grow if your property is not well maintained. If your place isn't immaculate, then you're losing business. All it takes is one bad online review to ruin your business.

Be proactive. Assemble a Team to assist you if maintenance is not one of your strengths. Interview local handymen with solid references who are willing to work within your budget. But, don't limit your search. Ask family, friends to assist or to refer other reliable individuals to assist with maintenance.

10 Tips on Maintaining your Vacation Rental Home

1. **Assemble a cleaning staff**: It may be a good idea to hire a cleaning consultant to come out and teach you and your staff a class. You will probably learn a lot of cleaning techniques and obtain additional info that will make the process a lot easier.

2. **Make a maintenance check list**: First compile a checklist of your property's needs. Then, make a list of all supplies needed to address your property's maintenance needs. The checklist will give you a clear idea of how much to budget.

3. **Use the right cleaning products**: Quality cleaning products should be used to properly clean and disinfect the home. Buy reputable products that get the job done. If you're working with a limited budget, test some of the off brands. Some work just as well if not better than popular

brands. Sanitizing and disinfecting beds and bedding are a must. I have found success using high quality cleaning products from Geogenex.

(www.FreedomGuide.Geogenex.com)

4. **Pay attention to details**: When maintaining your property, it's important to pay attention to all the big and little things. Guests look everywhere. They look in closets, under the bed, in drawers, behind furniture, and anywhere that catches their eye.

   The condition of your linen and beds should be on the top of your priority list. This is where guests lay their heads to get a good night's rest. The bedding should be clean, fresh, spot free and coordinated. There's nothing tackier than a makeshift set. Make sure everything goes together. If you're thinking about being creative, I recommend you play it safe and deliver something that won't warrant a red flag.

   Your home must be dust free and smell fresh. There's nothing like the first impression of a freshly sanitized and clean home. Dust free homes and clean homes show the guest that the property is well maintained. It's important that furniture is moved and areas that dirt and dust can assemble be removed. Because guests move furniture around, even if you tell them not too, it's important to clean hidden areas throughout your property. It's also important to keep dust to a minimum because some of your guest may have health conditions and you must keep a hazard free home for their health and safety.

5. **Equip the home with essentials**: There are many essentials that guest expect to be in your home. Ensuring that these items are in your home makes your guests stay more enjoyable and provides convenience. A coffee pot is one of the most requested items. A list of other recommended items is in "The Toolbox" in Step # 6 of this book.

6. **Manicure the interior**: A home manicure is when your home is neat, crisp, and everything is in its proper place. Remember that many vacationers inspect and closely observe many details of your property. So, do your best to fine-tune and pay attention to the little things. This will help you create a lasting impression with your guests.

7. **Suggestions**: Collate all your dishes in your cabinets neatly and orderly. Polish the silverware, metal appliances and cookware. Dust proof all the glassware. People appreciate clean and shiny items especially in the kitchen. They also value order. When items are out of order it can create a sense of confusion. The linen closet is a perfect example. All linen should be folded, separated, collated, and neatly placed in the linen closet.

8. **Manicuring the exterior**: A well-manicured lawn can make your guests feel like royalty.

9. **Exterminate**. Bed bugs and roaches are the kiss of death. A bug problem of any kind is a huge problem. Therefore, you must stay on top of your maintenance and regularly scheduled extermination schedule. You also should make a general practice to inspect and disinfect the beds after each booking. This literally means using a microscope. Bugs can hide in the seams of your bed, furniture, rugs, clothing, and linen. All your fabric materials are vulnerable. Frequent shampooing is also advised to avoid infestation.

    My vacation home rental property is in the desert of Las Vegas. There are a unique variety of bugs to contend with. Some crawl. Some fly. Some even kill. Getting a wake-up call from a Scorpion, Black Widow, or a Brown Recluse spider is not anyone's idea of a memorable vacation experience.

    Be certain to include instructions in your house rules with regards to garbage disposal procedures and food storage. This definitely will help avoid undesirable entry into your home of bugs and rodents.

10. **Wildlife Info**. Wild animals such as snakes, alligators, bears, mountain lions, sharks, coyotes, and raccoons are common habitat to some vacation hot spots. Popular tourist neighborhoods near the everglades of Florida,

the Pocono mountains of Pennsylvania, the desert mountains of Arizona, and the oceans of California in particular have reported their share of incidents involving humans and wild animals. In fact, many new subdivisions are built right in the heart of wildlife's habitat. Therefore, some incidences between man and nature are bound to occur.

Your guest should be provided with verbal and written instruction for preventive measures to avoid encounters with unfriendly wildlife. Here are some of the tips you can put in your policy and procedures to assist with keeping wildlife away from your property.

- Properly store food (especially outdoor food containment).
- Properly store other items that have a strong scent or odor (including removing Garbage Disposal excess).
- Actively look for and Read all signs pertaining to wildlife in the area.
- Speak to the lifeguard and read signs before swimming in the ocean at a beachfront property.

Supply your guests with all necessary storage equipment for inside and outdoor entertaining.

- Metal food storage boxers are great for backyards located in the mountains
- Coolers with locks
- Heavy duty garbage cans with locks

- Heavy duty garbage bags

Be certain to inform guests of the days and times for neighborhood garbage pick-up. Include this info in your house rules. Visibly post them as well as remind your guests of the importance of complying with these procedures.

You also need to clearly indicate, in your pet policy, what types of animals guests are allowed to bring to your property. Do not leave this to the interpretation of your guest. Some people have pet monkeys and many other types of animals. And, because they consider them to be a part of their family, they'll bring them along on their vacation. This is unless you clearly spell out your restrictions to them verbally and in writing.

Utility Conservation & Maintenance

One of the best cost-saving strategies for effectively managing your business is energy conservation. In the early stages of growing your business, every dollar counts. By closely monitoring you and your guest's usage of energy in your home, you'll save hundreds if not thousands of dollars per year.

Ten tips on energy conservation

1. Unplug appliances that don't need to be used such as televisions, microwaves, coffee makers, stereo, etc. If left plugged in, these appliances continue to use energy.

2. Minimize usage of your heating and air conditioning system. Turn the units off when the property is vacant.

3. Keep your programmable thermostat at 78 degrees in the summer months and 68 degrees in the winter months.

4. Seal all windows and doors for improved insulation. Weather strips and corking will prevent over usage of energy.

5. Install energy efficient light bulbs and solar powered lights.

6. Utilize the natural light in your home.

7. Assess your landscaping to make improvements that will maximize energy conservation. Don't be so quick to cut down trees. Some block a direct hit from the sun.

8. Turn off computers and office machinery that are not in use.

9. Buy energy efficient products for your home.

10. Post a "Going Green" policy in your welcome package and house rules. This will increase your guest's consciousness of energy saving practices during their stay in your home. Getting your guest to abide by some of the energy

saving practices will result in a direct savings and bigger profits for your vacation home rental business.

Keeping up with Repairs

Conducting routine checks of the condition and working order of all appliances and furnishings will save you a lot of time, money and headaches in the long run. It is recommended that you complete a thorough inspection after every booking to identify any damaged or broken items. In addition to keeping you fully abreast of any maintenance needed to your property, you also will minimize complaints from guests in knowing that every appliance and furnishing on your property is fully functional.

Tracking and recording all repairs with a Repair Log is a great idea to implement. It should include the dates of repairs and by whom those repairs were completed. Most repairs that are done outside the handyman can be expensive. Pick a reputable company that backs their work. Create an alliance. Making a preferred vendor friend will gain another participant in the B2B fan-club. The more business owners spread the good word, the better off your business will be.

On-Call Handyman

Accidents due occur. Breakers blow, toilets overflow, pipes leak, and many other problems can arise during a vacationers stay. Vacationers understand that things happen. You simply want to resolve the matter as quickly as possible and apologize for any inconvenience that it may have caused.

Having an on-call handyman and other vendors who are available 24 hours a day will assist with smoothly handling any emergencies that may arise. Visibly post a list of Emergency Contact telephone numbers and email addresses including your 24-hour vendors. This serves as a back-up in case guests are unable to reach you. You should also include this Emergency Contact list in the Welcoming Packet. Then, review all emergency procedures during your walk through.

Summary

Maintaining your home and property for the purpose of creating a successful vacation home rental business has its challenges. But, the *Freedom Guide* provides you with specific strategies that you can implement to proactively minimize any challenges. The comfort of your guests is important and so is their safety. As long as you never take these matters lightly, then you should do fine in properly maintaining your property and in handling all emergencies in a timely manner.

UTILIZE THE TOOLBOX RESOURCES

THE *Toolbox* is a chapter filled with informational tidbits, templates of essential forms and references to other websites and expert resources to assist you in running your business smoothly and efficiently. The *Freedom Guide* Toolbox gives you the blueprint that will give life to your business. The "Toolbox" holds all the equipment which brings together all of the remaining tools you'll need to get your business up and running. This chapter provides you with all of the forms, additional information, preferred websites and vendors that you'll need to utilize to get started.

For starters, with your purchase of the guide, you'll receive a lifetime membership to www.702vacationrentals.com. This site is an online matching service that will take reservations for your home. When 702vacationrentals.com calls you, you're already booked! This is just one of the tools I will introduce to you to secure vacation rental bookings. Most of these tools are free and only require a minimal amount of effort. Get ready to open your toolbox because it's loaded with all the tools you need to get going.

The sample forms in the toolbox are just that. They're samples. You're encouraged to utilize the samples provided in the toolbox to customize your own forms. What's most important is that you create a system that works best for you.

I'm not an attorney. So, it would also be a good idea to consult with one before duplicating and implementing any forms. The sole purpose of the samples is to give you an idea of what type of forms will be needed to operate your business. It's your job to customize the forms to fit your specific business needs.

Creating a format to customize your forms can be done in Microsoft Word. When constructing your documents and forms, make your best effort to cover all major points of concern. At the same time, keep your forms as short, sweet, and to the point as possible. Having your forms readily available to send out to prospective renters will assist you with reserving guests more quickly.

Your preparation and organization is very important. A large part of your interaction with renters is online. Therefore, it's important to have the ability to send out forms in just a click of your fingers. Being organized at your computer can save a lot of time and energy. The web has made it much easier to conduct business efficiently.

Try to get some of your paperwork completed and signed prior to the guest arriving. Guests generally dislike being bogged down with contracts, rules and regulations on the first day of their vacation. Presenting too much paperwork at check-in could possibly agitate your guests and be perceived as a hassle. Remember that your guests are ready for fun, sun and relaxation. The last thing they want to see is a bunch of paperwork.

Try to make the check-in and paperwork review process as fun and light as possible. Use humor to break the ice and to keep guest interested. Cover the most important details of your paperwork during your walk-thru, especially the fire safety and emergency evacuation policy. This will keep highlighted points of your homes policies fresh in their minds and much easier for them to remember. Once the walk thru is completed, they can easily start completing the paperwork.

SCRIPT

Hi, My name is_____

from _____.

I received an inquiry from
_____ in regards to the
dates you requested. I am delighted to tell you that your
dates are available.

_____

is a very special home. It features _____

_____

_____

_____

_____

_____

The home has a unique feel. It's inviting and warm. You
will love it.

Is this your first time in the area? This is a great place to vacation. There are many popular tourist attractions in the area.

How many people are you expecting in your party?

Are there any special needs or services that you and the other guest may need? We offer additional services such as

_____.

How soon are you looking to reserve your dates?

We are running a special promotion with discounted rates. If you reserve today, you will get _____ percent off your total stay.

The total cost including all fees and the discount is $_____.

This is a great offer that will save you over _____ dollars off our seasonal rate.

I am e-mailing you the agreement and house rules.

Which credit card would you like to use?

We also accept PayPal. I will send over a request for payment.

Confirmation of Reservation

Once accepting a booking, a confirmation form should be sent via e-mail. Collect payment after you receive the completed form. Give guests the option of mailing, faxing or emailing the completed form to you. Either way, make sure the form is completed and signed. Below is a sample of a Confirmation of Reservation form:

Enclosed are our rental agreement and house rules. Please read carefully, print, sign and send it along with a 50% deposit of the total rental amount. Thank you and if you have any questions, please feel free to call me.

Thank you

Cathy Burch, Desert Charm Estates

Today's date
Your Address
Your city, state, and zip code
Your phone number
e-mail info@desertcharmestate.com
www.desertcharmestate.com

Sample Rental Agreement/Contract

LENGTH OF STAY_____

RATES

Rental rates for Desert Charm Estates are located on the reservation page.

TAXES

CLEANING

$_____

PAYMENT

All payments under $2,500 are due at the time of reservation.

REFUNDS/CANCELLATIONS

Should you decide to cancel your booking after we have received your rental check, and we are unable to re-rent, your deposit will be entirely forfeited. We are not able to trade or bank your booked dates for another time in the future.

CHECK IN - OUT

Check-In time 3:00 p. m. Check-out time 10:00 a. m. Check- outs beyond 10 a.m. are subject to penalties.

LATE CHECK-OUTS

Check-out is 10:00 a.m. sharp. If available, you may request a late check-out, up to 5:00 p. m., provided we have no guest checking in the day of your departure. You must arrange this in advance with your agent. The late check-out fee is $150. This option is popular with Sunday football fans.

DAMAGES

Security Deposits are partially refundable or kept entirely for the following reasons.

1. Cancelling booking within 3 weeks of expected visit.

2. Undeclared pets.

3. Undeclared large events, such as weddings.

4. Signs of smoking inside the home. Smoking is permitted only outside the home.

5. Excessive cleaning required over staff's normal 4 hour visit.

6. A $55 fee will be assessed for any missing remote controls.

7. Late check-outs in excess of two hours will be billed at $150.

GRIEVANCES

All Grievances will be handled by Management.

FURNISHINGS

All properties are equipped and furnished to the owner's taste and are set-up for light housekeeping. Mattress

Pads, pillows, blankets and bedspreads are provided. Tenant is responsible to pay replacement of any furnishings, linens, fixtures or equipment that is damaged during their stay.

MAINTENANCE AND REPAIRS

We make every effort to ensure that all equipment within each rental is in working order. In the event of a breakdown, we will strive to repair it as soon as possible after being notified of a problem. We cannot guarantee that spas, televisions, appliances, high-speed access, etc. will not break down during your stay and therefore, no refunds or adjustments will be made for mechanical failure. Furthermore, there will be no refunds or adjustments made for any other unexpected situation beyond our control such as bugs, rodents, weather and the like.

SECURITY OF THE HOME

When you lease the home, you assume full responsibility for it and its contents, as well as your personal property. Always lock the doors and windows when you leave. Lock your automobiles and put away any rental equipment.

MONTHLY RENTALS

All rentals must be paid in advance

LOST ITEMS

While we will do our best to accommodate you within 2 weeks with items left behind, you are responsible for anything left at the home. Please be sure to pack all of your belongings. Neither Agent nor Owner is responsible for lost, stolen, or abandoned items. There will be a fee plus shipping for any found and returned items.

MAIL

Packages and mail can be received by guest with prior approval. No acceptance of the primary tenants mail or packages by guest.

CATERING

Desert Charm Estate's contracted catering service must cater all events. Rates & Menus can be faxed or emailed. Outside catering events are prohibited.

HOUSE RULES WILL BE STRICTLY ENFORCED.

ALL REVIEWS will be submitted to Management in Writing and not posted on Online.

Main Renter's name

_____

Number of guests_____

Rental Amount_____

Check in date_____

Check out date_____

Freedom Guide forms are available at www.fdguide.com

Sample Welcoming Package

Welcoming Packages should include the following:

- Welcome letter

- Policies and Procedures

- Rules & Regulations

- A copy of the guest signed agreement

- Management contact information

- Floor plan

- Brochures and information for nearby activities and events

Sample of Welcome Letter

DEAR GUEST:

Thank You for choosing Desert Charm Estates for your accommodations in Las Vegas. Please feel free to let us know if you need anything.

We would appreciate it if you would take the time to fill out the Check-In paperwork and review the house rules. Our mission at Desert Charm Estates is for our guests to have a positive and memorable experience.

Thank You and enjoy your stay.

Ms. Cathy Burch

Guest Coordinator

Desert Charm Estate

702 704-9909

info@desertcharmestate.com

Basket Items are a Great Welcoming Gift

Gift basket: Disposable cameras, chocolates, beverages, crackers, cheeses, assorted meats, bottles of sauces,

Spa basket: Bath scrubs, bubble bath, sponge, scented lotions, scented candles, body spray, and organically scented soaps.

Fruit basket: assorted fruits, assorted cheeses, assorted crackers, breads, and candies

Other Suggested Gift items

Disposable Cameras	T-Shirts
Coffee Mugs	Pens
Key Chains	Twin Champagne Glasses
Gift Card	Assorted Candies

Sample Check-In & Check-Out Procedure
Desert Charm Estates

1. All the rooms must be in clean condition and acceptable accommodations for guest (Guest Sign Acceptance Form).

2. All appliances and furnishings are in working order. Guest signs acceptance form.

3. The names and license plate #'s of all guests are to be documented.

4. Guests are given house rules verbally and sign attestation form stating they will abide by the rules.

5. Guests are given emergency contact information.

6. Both the guest coordinator and the guests will tour all the rooms and note any discrepancies and complaints (refer to attestation form).

7. Guests are given notice that all complaints will be handled as soon as possible and normally within 24 hours.

8. Guest Coordinator must be present for check-out and allowed to inspect property on a daily basis if necessary.

9. Complaint/Damage Report needs to be filled out at check-in or check-out if Applicable.

Check —In Attestation Form

I_____ accept the condition

of the Estate at check-in _____2011.

Time_____

It is mutually understood that both parties agree during check-in that the home was in clean and acceptable condition. All appliances are in working order. All complaints have been noted during the walk thru and will be resolved as soon as possible

Primary Guest Signature_____

Date_____

Guest Coordinator _____

Date_____

Freedom Guide forms are available at www.fdguide.com

Check-Out Form

Time_____

Primary Guest Coordinator

_____

Damages_____

Missing Items_____

Condition of Flooring

_____

Condition of Furnishings

_____

Condition of Appliances

_____

Structural Damage_____

Other_____

It is mutually understood by both parties that if there are any damages, missing items or violations of the house rules, this will automatically result in a forfeit of the security deposit. If such violations are discovered after check-out, the guest will be notified via telephone, email or regular mail.

Guest_____

Date_____

Guest Coordinator_____

Date_____

Freedom Guide forms are available at www.fdguide.com

Testimonials

In an effort to ensure quality service at Desert Charm Estate, we would greatly appreciate your feedback in regards to your stay.

Cleanliness

_____

_____

_____

_____

Staff Assistance

_____

_____

_____

_____

Other

_____

_____

_____

_____

Thank you for your feedback. The management and staff at Desert Charm Estates want to make all of our guests stay memorable. Your comments are appreciated.

Guest Information

Primary Renter_____

Guest 1_____

Guest 2_____

Guest 3_____

Guest 4_____

Guest 5_____

Guest 6_____

Guest 7_____

Guest 8_____

Guest 9_____

___

Guest 10_____

Visiting Guests

_____

_____

_____

_____

_____

Please indicate the names and ages of all children
specifically

Name_____Age_____

Name_____Age_____

Name_____Age_____

It is mutually understood that both parties understand that the guest count is limited to 16 overnight guest and 20 person occupancy. Any violation of this will result in an event rate being charged and a forfeit of the deposit.

Primary Guest Signature_____

Date _____

Guest Coordinator_____

Date_____

Freedom Guide forms are available at www.fdguide.com

Vehicle Form

1. Vehicle Make/
   Model_____

   Plate #_____

2. Vehicle Make/
   Model_____

   Plate #_____

3. Vehicle Make/
   Model_____

   Plate #_____

4. Vehicle Make/
   Model_____

   Plate #_____

Additional Vehicles _____

House Rules

The home must be left clean at check out.

The renters must abide by the capacity designated by the rental agreement.

Any violation of capacity will result in an event charge and a forfeit of the security deposit.

No loud music.

Any disruptive or violent behavior will result in the authorities being called.

No unauthorized parties.

Do not remove or move the accessories or furnishings.

All garbage must be properly bagged, secured and left curbside or at a designated area for pick-up. Pick-up days and times are clearly posted.

Any damages to the home structure, furnishings, flooring or items in the home outside normal wear and tear will result in a forfeit of the deposit and possibly additional charges.

Children are not allowed to swim in pool unattended.

An additional fee will be charged for excessive usage of utilities.

No entry to locked or unauthorized areas.

Check-outs are required with a guest coordinator.

A Late Check-out is an additional fee.

All keys and garage door openers must be returned at check-out. If keys are not returned, the deposit will be forfeited.

All deposits will be returned within 30 days if applicable.

The staff at Desert Charm Estate has the right to conduct daily inspections.

Any violation of the above house rules will forfeit the security deposit and may require additional fees.

Enjoy Your Stay!

Management

Pet Policy

1. Dogs & Cats only.
2. Dogs must be house broken.
3. All dogs must be treated with repellent at least 3 days before arrival.
4. Owner is responsible for the care and maintenance of their pet.
5. More than one pet will require an additional fee of $300.00.
6. Owner will forfeit their entire deposit if any damages occur from their pet.
7. Exotic pets prohibited.
8. Owners must submit current vaccination records prior to arrival.
9. Dogs must be leashed at all times.
10. The homeowner does not assume responsibility for any injury or illness to a renter's pet that may occur while being on the premises.
11. Pet owners are responsible for cleaning up pet feces and all other refuse.

Fire and Evacuation Policy

1. In case of Fire call 911.
2. Turn off stove and ovens after usage.
3. Please turn off all appliances after usage.
4. Make sure all candles are blown out.
5. Smoking is prohibited inside the home.
6. Ash trays must be used outside of the home.
7. All fire extinguisher locations must be posted.
8. Roll down ladders are available in second floor & upper level closets for emergency exiting.
9. Floor plans are posted in designated hallways.
10. All exits must be highlighted on floor plan and physically marked during the walk thru.
11. All unused outlets must remain plugged with plastic covers.
12. Please notify staff if smoke detectors or carbon dioxide units are inoperable.

Emergency Contact

These are the telephone numbers that should be posted in a visible area such as the kitchen or near the front door.

1. Vacation Rental Owners
2. Handyman
3. 24 Hour Plumbers
4. Nearest Hospital
5. 24 Hour Electrician
6. Property Management

In case of Emergency, the guests will be able to get in touch with vendors. Unforeseen issues such as excessive water leaks, electrical problems or other maintenance issues may arise.

Normally the owner or the property management will initiate contact with vendors, but if the guest for some odd reason are unable to contact the owner, having the list visible could assist them in controlling damages and effectively handling any emergency situation.

Security Procedure

1. Keep doors locked.
2. Close and lock all windows after use.
3. Close and lock garage doors after use.
4. Activate burglar alarm before leaving the home.
5. Deactivate burglar alarm once re-entering the home.
6. Notify management of any unauthorized persons visiting the home.
7. Notify management of any suspicious activity.
8. Call 911 in case of emergency.

Utility Usage Policy

Turn off all lights when leaving the home.

Turn off all appliances when not in use.

Set thermostat at 78 degrees in the summer months and 68 degrees in the winter months.

Close all windows and doors.

Excessive and unnecessary usage of utilities will result in an extra charge and a possible hold on your security deposit until the next billing cycle.

Pool Policy

Call 911 in case of a medical emergency.

1. All children must be monitored and supervised while using the pool.
2. All children and inexperienced swimmers must use life preservers.
3. Adults' swimming alone is at your own risk.
4. No drinking alcohol while swimming.
5. All heating units for spa and pool must be shut off after usage.
6. No horseplay or dunking in the pool.
7. No pushing others in the pool.
8. All guests must be aware of where the first-aid kit is located.
9. Supervising individual must be certified or be able to perform CPR.
10. The owner is not responsible for any injuries that may occur during usage of the pool on the premises.

Freedom Guide forms are available at www.fdguide.com

Recommended Items

Broom	cake pans
Mop	muffin pans
Dust Pan	Cookie sheets
Blender	cover plastic bowl set
Cutting Board	four slice toaster
Can Opener	strainer
Cork Screw	measuring spoon
Microwave	measuring cup
Toaster oven	butcher knife set
Mixer	skillet
Cutting board	crock -pot
Fire extinguisher	portable storage closet
Variety of batteries	plug covers
Coffee Maker (auto off)	first aid kit
Tea kettle	hair dryer
Vegetable peeler	board games
Children's plastic plate sets	Juicer
Plastic pitcher	PC Printer/fax
Nut cracker	ice cream scooper

Cookbooks	BBQ Grill
Outdoor grilling utensils	TV Guide
Door Mat	picnic basket
Outdoor candles	flash light
Mending kit	bubble bath
His & Her White Robs	His & Her Slippers
Plastic Spatula	waste baskets
Plastic/metal slotted spoon	lighters
Tongs	Blender
Plungers	Pooper scooper
Internet	Cable
Universal cell phone chargers	Printer
Fax Machine	Shredder
Scanner	

Dinnerware

Plates	water glasses
Bowls	tea glasses
Salad bowls	wine glasses
Saucers	cups
Tea glasses	mugs

Tablespoons	rock glasses
Teaspoons	Punch Bowls
Tablespoons	Glass Pitcher
Steak knives	Martini glasses
Dinner folks	Stainless Shaker
Salad folks	Punch fountain
Chop sticks	Fondue set

Cookware

The easy way to supply your cookware for you vacation rental is to purchase a 16-18 Piece Stainless steel Cookware Set.

Purchase additional pieces that will compliment your set. Get duplicates of the most frequently used pieces such as frying pans and 4", 6" and 8" inch pots.

Miscellaneous

DVD Player	CD Player
VCR	waste baskets
Universal Remotes	Alarm Clocks
Blankets	Reading Lamps
Feather Beds	Plug in wall lights

Air Mattresses	Humidifier
Pillow Protectors	New Tooth Brushes
Mattress Protectors	Pot holders
Pillows	pot warmers
Ashtrays	Place mats
Coasters	Napkin Holder
Irons	Cake Cover
Local phone book	Water toys
Ironing boards	Pet Toys

Recommended Cleaning Supplies

Pine	Laundry Detergent
Bleach	Fabric Softener
Air freshener Cones	Leather cleaner
Fabric Deodorizers	Degreaser
Marble & Granite Cleaner	Tile Cleaner
Dishwasher Detergent	All Purpose Cleaner
Furniture polish	Dishwashing liquid
Orange oil	Dust Cleaner
Toilet cleaner	Sanitizing wipes
Stainless steel cleaner	Plug In

Streak free window cleaner	Wet jets
Carpet & spot cleaner	oven cleaner
Carpet deodorizer	stove cleaner
Tub scrubber	Grout Cleaner

Brochures and Information

Maps

Menus

Show Brochures

Park locations

Shopping information

Coupons for discount attractions and tours

Local Spas

Security Gate info

Directions to the nearest hospital

WEBSITES

Social Media Websites

Facebook.com	Twitter.com
Myspace.com	Mylife.com
Flickr.com	Affluence.com
Linkedin.com	Tagged.com
Nexopia.com	Bepo.com
H5.com	Hyves.com
Studio v.com	Nasza.com
Decayenne.com	Tagged.com
Xing.com	Badoo.com
Skyrock.com	Orkut.com
Friendship.com	Mixi.com
Skorpypluxuryclub.org	Aubers.com
Affluence.org	Whiptunes.com

Vacation Rental Blogs

Newletter.blizzardinternet.com

Cottageblogger.com

Blogflipkey.com

Free Networking Websites for Vacation Rental Owners

Yahoovacationrentalgroups.com

Laymyhat.com

Preferred Free Websites

Flipkey.com

Rentalspot.com

Rentmyspace.com

Free-rentals.com

Vivium.com

Domegos.com

Kijiji.com

Vivium.com

Search4rentals.com

Scenicrentals.com

Householidays.com

Rental365.com

Gullivers.com

Staysite.com

Findyourvacationhome.com

Share-house.com

ebayclassified.com

Rentals.com

Getawaydigs.com

Arrangeyourvacation.com

Alwaysonvacation.com

Vacationpads.com

BVoML.com

Rentalexpress.com

Gayvacationrentals.com

Vacationrentalhub.com

Gayplaces2rent.com

Sea2seavacationrental.com

Hotstays.com

Hotpads.com

Tourist-paradise.com

e-vacation-homerentals.com

vacationrentalads.com   houserentals.us.com

tree-houseforrent.com   findmyroof.com

10000vacations.com   Hotelforall.com

Lookvacationrentals.com   Groupaccommodations.com

Vamoose.com   Pickmyvacationrental.com

Planetvacationrentals.com   Idealdigs.com

Vacationrentalconnection.com

Preferred Free-International Websites

holidayworldwidedirect.com   anunico.us.com

topchoicevacationrental.com   holidaylettings.com

vacation-rental-wonderland.com   holidayrentals.co.uk

homevacationrentals.com   airbnb.com

Free Classified Websites

Integiant.com   Freeads8.com

Superads.com   Usfreeads.com

Adsglobe.com   Admyclassified.com

Adpost.com   Classifiedforfree.com

Recycler.com   Ep.com

Classifiedyahoo.com   1second.com/1americ.htm

Impa.com

Holton.com

Il-monti.com

Freeclassified.com

Dollarads.com

Comcorner.com

Adsbynet.com

Classifiedtoday.com

Bestmall.com

Messageboardblaster.com

Ablewise.com

admaxpro.com

classifiedclub.com

http:/annonz.co.uk

http:/www.livedeal.com

http:/theadnet.com

Citynews.com

Axfamily.com/class

Theadnet.com

Ad2go.com

Epage.com

4-1-1.com/ads/newad.html

Networkedclassified.com

Webovation.com

Freebizadsweb.com

Oims.com

http://johannesbug.gum

adlandpro.com

http:/www.usnetads.com

www.google.com/base

http:/classifiedforfree.com

http:/te.co.nz/

www.nzdirectory.conz/ads/index.php

http:/cracker.com.au/

http://australia.zeezo.com/classified-adshtmree.coza/

Recommended Free Matching Websites (Commissions)

702VacationRentals.com   OwnersDirect.com

Redawning.com   airbnb.com

Free Ads

Leadspider.com   craigslist.com

Olx.com   Tedslist.com

Recycler.com   Suppershopper.com

Gayellowpages.com   Gaylesbiandirectory.com

EBay classified   backpage.com

Free Websites to Advertise for Small Gatherings/Parties or Weddings

Eventective.com

Website's that Advertise Last-Minute Deals

Licketytrip.com   Howtovacation.com

Clearstay.com   Forgetaway.com

Lastminuterental.com   Valuevacationrental.com

House Swap Websites

Tradetotravel.com   Pad4Pad.com

Craigslist.com (for best results, post ads in surrounding states every 48 hrs.)

Recommended Websites with Fees

VRBO.com

Homeaway.com

Rentalo.com

Vacationhomerental.com

Rentcap.com

Paradisehunter.com

Keyvacationrentals.com

Findvacationrental.com

Vivium.com

Myholidayhomerental.com

Firstvacations.com

Idealvacationrentals.com

Onlinevacationrentals.com

Vacationrental.org

Travelehome.com

VacationRentalPeople.com

Masterpiecerentals.com

Wimdu.com

VRWD.com

Vacationrentals.com

chbo.com

Vacationhome.com

Directvacationrentals.com

Vrconnections.com

Perfictplaces.com

Vacationrentalslisted.com

Greatvacations.com

Cyberrentals.com

Vacationrentalspaces.com

Timeawayrentals.com

Rentcap.com

Idealvacationrentals.com

HomeGetaways.com

Trulia.com

LivingSocial.com   LivingSocialEscapes.com

Perfictplaces.com   Vacationrentalslisted.com

Myholidayhomerental.com   Greatvacations.com

Firstvacations.com   Cyberrentals.com

Idealvacationrentals.com   Vacationrentalspaces.com

Family Friendly

Greatfamilyrentals.com

Luxury Rental Websites

The society.com   Dreamexoticrentals.com

Luxury-retreats.com   Carefreelifestyle.com

Jetsetters.com

Charity Vacation Rental Websites

Geronimo.com   Estatevacationrentals.com

Pet Friendly Vacation Home Rental Sites

Petfriendlytravel.com

Recommended Cleaning Products

www.FreedomGuide.Geogenex.com

Video Websites

Youtube.com   Justin.tv

tubemogul   Instagram.com

Poker Player Websites

suitedcribs.com

Lasvegashomevacationrentals.com

Golf Player Websites

Golfcribs.com   Back9rentals.com

Free Website Development

Wix.com

Yola.com

Preferred Website Designer

Designvibe.com

Loan Modification Advocate Group

NACA (Neighborhood Assistance Corporation of America) is an Advocacy group that assists individuals in negotiating with mortgage companies and applying for loan modifications. NACA also provides a forensic audit to determine if any violations occurred in obtaining your current mortgage (www.NACA.com).

Government Loan Modification Program

MakingYourHomeAffordable.gov

Incorporating Services (Registering the business)
Nevada Corporation or LLC

http://www.nchaffiliate.com/freedomguide/config.php

Business Consulting Services

www.ntmsolutions.com

SCORE (www.score.org)

No Cost or Low Cost Furniture

Craigslist	Goodwill
Salvation Army	Factory Direct
Used Hotel Furniture Outlets	Garage Sales
Swap Meets	

State Sales Tax Offices

These are the contacts for collecting and paying sales tax.

Alabama
www.ador.state.us/sales/index.html

Alaska
www.dced.state.ak.us/dca/LOGON/tax/tax-sales.htm

Arizona
www.revenue.state.az.us

California
www.boe.ca.gov/sutax/faqscont.htm

Colorado
www.revenue.state.co.us/TPS-Dir/wrap.asp?incl=shtml

Connecticut
www.ct.gov

Delaware
www.state.de.us/revenue/index.htm

Florida
www.myflorida.com/dor/taxes/sales-html

Georgia
www2.state.ga.us/departments/dor/salestax/index.shtml

Hawaii
www.state.hi.us/tax

Idaho
www2.state.id.us/tax/questions.htm

Illinois
www.revenue.state.il.us

Indiana
www.ai.org/dor/taxforms/s-wforms.html

Iowa
www.state.ia.us/tax/taxlaw/taxtypes.html#sales

Kansas
www.ksrevenue.org

Kentucky
www.krevenue.org

Louisiana
www.rev.state.la.us/sections/business/sales.asp#sales

Maine
www.state.me.us/revenue/salesanduse/homepage.html

Maryland
www.business.marylandtaxes.com/taxinfo/salesanduse/default.
asp

Massachusetts
www.dor.state.ma.us/help/guide/stg-form.htm

Michigan
www.michigan.gov/treasury

Minnesota
www.taxes.state.mn.us/taxes/sales/index.shtml

Mississippi
www.mstc.state.ms/taxeareas/sales/main.htm

Montana
www.discoveringmontana.com/revenue/css3forbusiness/01taxe
slicensesfees/g-salestax/default.asp

Nebraska
www.revenue.state.ne.us/salestax/htm

Nevada
www.tax.state.nv.us

New Hampshire
www.state.nh.us./treasury/meals+ rentals/index/htm

New Jersey
www.state.nj.us/treasury/taxation/index

New Mexico
www.statenm.us./tax

New York
www.tax.state.ny.us/forms/sales-cur-forms.htm

North Carolina
www.dor.state.nc.us/taxes/sales

North Dakota
www.state.dd.us/taxdpt/salessanduse

Ohio
www.tax.ohio.gov/business_taxes_sales.html

Oklahoma
www.oktax.state.ok.us/btforms.html

Oregon
www.dor.state.or.us

Pennsylvania
www.revenue.state.pa.us/revenue/taxonomy/taxonomy.aspDLN

Rhode Island
www.tax.state.ri.us/info/synopsis/syntoc.htm

South Carolina
www2.sc.tax.org/sales

South Dakota
www.state.sd.usl2/Revenue.html

Tennessee
www.state.tn.us/revenue/tntaxes/salesanduse.htm

Texas
www.window.state.tx.us/taxinfo/sales/new-business.html

Utah
www.tax.utah.gov./sales/index.html

Vermont
www.state.vt.us/tax/index.htm

Virginia
www.tax.state.va.us/site.cfm?alias=SalesUseTax

Washington
http://dor.wa.gov/content/findtaxesandrates/
salesandusetaxrates/lookupataxrate/

Washington DC
www.gov/index.asp

West Virginia
www.state.wv.us/taxdiv

Wisconsin
www.dor.state.wi.us/html/taxsales.html

Wyoming
www.revenue.state.wsy.us/doclistout.asp?div=12&dtype=6

Tips on How to Make a Friend

You may naturally be a friendly person. But, in business, I've learned that it's best to have a clear strategy and approach to market your business. I'm not suggesting you fake being genuine in forming friendships. But, this strategic move can greatly enhance your marketing efforts. Below are some helpful tips:

Making a friend is making a fan.

1. Reach out to your friend immediately after receiving the inquiry. Via telephone and e-mail is the most common way to reach out to your inquirer. It's important to respond promptly. Some research suggests that contacting your inquirer within 3 hours can increase your chances of booking the reservation by 50%. This shows the vacationer that you're interested and that their vacation needs are a high priority.

2. Address the Vacationer by their first name with all correspondence. Addressing them by their first name suggests familiarity and makes them feel a little more relaxed.

3. Get all the necessary information such as the estimate, agreement, house rules, check-in and check-out procedure over to them as soon as you can. Getting information to the vacationer promptly will impress them. It's a great start! Time is of the essence. Travelers must secure their accommodations for their vacation. Keep in

mind what they're thinking and the fact that they may have sent other owners inquiries. Other owners are right behind you jockeying for position. Getting all the information over to the potential guest enables them to make the decision faster. And, a faster decision means the faster you'll see the money.

4. Make sure you address all the vacationers concerns in all correspondence. Address all their needs and inform them on how you can assist in servicing them.

5. Put the sell on them. Let them know all the great features of your property without sounding too pitchy. Address the ones that they are most interested in first and then give additional info on the ones that might interest them. Making suggestions never hurts unless you're way off base.

6. Find out what you and the vacationer have in common. Something may come up during your correspondence that you may be able to have an extended conversation about. Something you might have in common or can laugh about. It's always good to make the client laugh and feel good.

7. Make your client feel special. One of the biggest concerns of vacationers is price. If their ready to reserve but price is becoming the issue, find out what their budget is and

see if you can make the deal happen. The last thing you want to happen is that you lose a deal over a differential of a very small amount of money. "Remember fast nickels are better than slow dimes". Once the client feels that you are flexible to work within his or her budget if it's within reason then you are on your way to really making a friend. I didn't say giveaway the kitchen sink. I'm just suggesting for you to make a Friend. Make them feel like they got the best deal ever. They don't have to know that the cleaning fee was inflated a little and that the deal was right at your bottom line anyway. Make them feel you worked it out especially for them. I can't say it enough. "Fast nickels are better than slow dimes".

8. Follow-up in a timely manner. You will find that the client will appreciate your prompt response and concern. Follow-up time should be called bonding time. By the time the deal is closed your vacationer should feel just as good about your customer service as they do about the anticipated experience at your home. Remember they are buying into both. Your salesmanship is a major part of the package.

9. Answer all questions. Giving your potential guest accurate information in a timely matter is important. If you don't know the answer to some of their questions, let them know you will get right back to them with the information. Being readily available to assist your guest

demonstrates that you can be valuable and instrumental in their travel plans. Be the concierge and the tourist information center for your client. It's just another hat you will be expected to wear. Wear it proudly and make your best effort to sell them on the total package which as an added bonus includes your knowledge. You will make a friend, and people do business with people who they perceive to be their friend. You will find yourself walking your client through the reservation process. Pointing the traveler in the right direction gains big points with potential guests. It shows that you care about their experience and that you want it to be just as great as they imagined.

10. Grab your telemarketing hat. Sounding confident, persuasive, and informative on the phone will gain you many friends. Applying all of the 9 other tips, along with your telemarketing/telesales skills and techniques will make you very successful. It all starts with the rapport on the phone and emails. People can be sold over the phone. Agency's do it every day to sell their product and services. You can do it too, by making a friend. Make sure your voice sounds confident and that it comes across that you know for sure what you're talking about. No stuttering, babbling, or usage of profanity. People like to be reassured that the salesperson is confident, knowledgeable and professional. Change the tone of your voice to put emphasis on certain words, phrases and information that you want to be received by your vacationer. *I am*

suggesting the usage of a customized script. This will remind you to hit all of your selling points in your efforts to constructively build the value by phone or in person every time.

Be persuasive with positive re-enforcements. Let them know about the positive experience of other guests. Tell them how much fun they're going to have. Give them a visual and something to get excited about. Paint a picture of what their experience will be with your words.

Be informative. Answer all the questions and be helpful. They will appreciate your effort.

Don't talk too fast and speak clearly when leaving messages on voice mail. This is especially important when you're leaving a return telephone number. Make sure you slowly repeat your name and number at least two times.

9 Tips to Achieving Successful Results with Telemarketing/ Telesales of a Vacation Rental

In this business it's all about the phone work

1. Plan before your call. Lay it out and think it out before you dial.

2. Effective communication. You must grab your prospective client's attention.

3. Question your prospective vacation renter. Find out what their needs are.

4. Show and build the value. Believe in the quality and value of the experience that they will have in renting your home.

5. Avoid Unnecessary Conversation. Make your best effort to focus on the product or service.

6. Avoid being pushy and aggressive. A hard sale is not appropriate for the vacation home rental business. Vacationers are buying into an expected experience and your role is to convey your vacation home rental in a package appetizing and desirable that will match what they envision. This will not be accomplished with a hard sale.

7. Avoid Harassing or being perceived as a pest.

8. Confronting clients that are indecisive. If your prospective vacationer seems like they can't come to a decision, then you may have to give them a gentle nudge. Let them know the consequences for failing to lock-in their reservation. Remind them that there could be a rate change or that there are other interested parties, etc.

9. Overcoming objectives. This is one of the hardest things professional salespeople face every day.

I know this may seem like a lot to do at first, but after a few conversations, it will come naturally. You will find yourself doing most of these things without thinking about it. Utilizing these strategies will give you more favorable results.

Summary

The roadmap to generating a positive cash flow from a vacation home rental ends here. Throughout this book, we've provided you with a step-by-step guide to starting your vacation home rental business on a solid legal foundation and minimizing the liabilities associated with establishing your own business. This book provides you with a broad overview of the vacation rental industry and how to successfully operate and manage a vacation home rental business. Thus, the *Freedom Guide* is a complete guide to creating a successful vacation home rental business.

The instructions, provided in the *Freedom Guide*, along with the easy to use forms in the toolbox, will lead you to financial relief and freedom. The *Freedom Guide* will also motivate and empower you to change your financial landscape. This book will show you how to set-up your home for business. And, it will provide you with critical insight to understanding what is most important to your guests so that you can meet and exceed their expectations.

The foundation upon which you build your business is a commitment to delivering what you advertise and providing the highest quality of customer service to your guests at all times. And, the *Freedom Guide* equips you for many of the challenges with which you'll be confronted in owning and operating a vacation home rental business. We provide a snapshot of scenarios that can occur and simple strategies that you can utilize to deal with them appropriately and in a timely manner.

The chapter on marketing informs and teaches the reader how to network, cultivate business relationships and gain visibility for their vacation rental online and offline. It also clearly illustrates how this can be accomplished for a low cost investment or no cost at all. Additionally, a wide range of ideas were presented for offering incentives to your guests, effectively connecting with vacationers and getting them to buy into your brand. So, all that's left to do now is begin enjoying the rewards of freedom.

ENJOY THE REWARDS OF FREEDOM

Rewards

THE *Freedom Guide* shows you how to enter the multibillion dollar travel industry as a vacation home rental owner with little or no start-up costs. Despite the peaks and valleys of the economy, the travel industry is here to stay. People will always want and need to take vacations and getaways. Even more, they now are searching for more creative and non-traditional vacation experiences. Thus, there are more opportunities than ever for you to use your home to reap the benefits of this growing trend.

In Step #1 "Motivation," we shared with you the unlimited opportunities that are available for you to transform your home into a vacation home rental. And, one of the key incentives is that you can pay your mortgage in a weekend. As we near the end of this book, I want to reemphasize how realistic it is for you to actually pay your mortgage in a weekend. The "Common Sense Analysis" table that we showed you in the opening chapter is displayed once again because it's such a powerful illustration.

Let's Do the Math
Sally Paid Her Mortgage in a Weekend

Sally has a $700 per month Mortgage.

She lives in Phoenix, Arizona.

Sally owns a 3 bedroom 1,300 square feet home.

She rents her home for $200 per night.

The Davis family from Iowa booked a reservation to stay at Sally's residence for 3 nights. The negotiated rate of payment was $200 per night for 3 nights + a $100 Cleaning Fee.

Sally in one weekend earned $700 which enabled her to pay her mortgage.

Common Sense Analysis

Estimates of Nightly Vacation Rental Rates

<u>Apartments/Condos</u> (per night)

Studio Apt.

($150-$250) + $200 cleaning fee X 3 days = $650-$950

1 bedroom Apt

($175- $300) + $200 cleaning fee X 3 days = $725-$1,100

2 bedroom Apt

($225-$350) + $225 cleaning fee X 3 days = $900-$1,275

3 bedroom Apt

($275-$425) + $225 cleaning fee X 3 days = $1,050-$1,500

Homes (per night)

Up to 1400 sq ft

($225 – $425 + $200 cleaning fee) X 3 days = $875-1,475

1500 to 2500 sq ft

($450-$500 + $200 cleaning fee) X 3 days = $1,550-1,700

2700 to 3500 sq ft

($525-$600 + $250 cleaning fee) X 3 days = $1,825-$2,050

4000 to 5500 sq ft

($600-$750 + $275 cleaning fee) X 3 days = $2,075-$2,525

6000 to 8000 sq ft

($850-$2,500 + $450 cleaning fee) X 3 days = $3,000-$7,950

*Pricing for all the following Accommodation Rates can vary at owner's discretion.

The opportunities that go along with entrepreneurship are endless. More money. Less taxes. More investment opportunities. The process of turning your home into a resort will not only make you a better business person. It will open the door to greater financial freedom.

Paid Mortgage and Utilities

The best perk of all is having my mortgage and utilities paid by the income I generate from vacation rentals. And, on top of it, my home pays me a little something extra. I love it!!!

Money for Investment Opportunities

Now that you're free you can start shopping for investments. Maybe it's time for you to capitalize on the bubble burst and pick up some properties. You might decide to turn them into a resort as well. Investing in long-term investments and letting the power of compound interest do its job is another great option. Or, you might decide to set up a trust fund for your children's education. Whatever investments you decide, this business will reward you by providing you with the means to pursue any investment strategy.

More Cash Flow for Financial Stability and Security

Creating additional cash flow is freedom in and of itself. The extra income provides you with a realistic avenue for charting a path towards financial freedom. Start with small goals like starting or increasing your emergency fund. Then, work towards larger goals like working full-time, without any financial strain, as a vacation home rental owner.

House Swapping Participation Programs

There are plenty of house swapping programs in which you can register or enroll your home. Now, I hardly ever book a hotel room. There's no need when there's a home in every part of the world that's offering home swapping. This is totally cost effective for me and just one of the many perks of being in the business.

The ultimate goal is to make your mortgage in a weekend. But, it's equally important to wisely manage the additional income that you soon will begin to generate. Things are going to start happening very fast, and managing the daily business will require additional time and energy on your part. That's why it's going to be very important to have a clear budget and financial plan in place to ensure that you continually improve your financial status and not repeat any mistakes you may have made in the past with regards to healthy budgeting and money management habits. For one, I strongly recommend hiring an inexpensive bookkeeper to organize your monthly receipts or utilize bookkeeping software. Secondly, I also recommend reading money management and financial investment books by financial advisors such as Suze Orman. I can show you how to make lots of money - your mortgage in a weekend - by using the Freedom Guide, but I'm not a financial expert.

The bestselling book *The Millionaire Next Door* by Thomas Stanley and William Danko paints a vivid picture that the wealthiest people are not necessarily the most extravagant people. They are definitely hard working people like you and I. They've just decided to spend smarter and invest wiser. They've learned the secret to controlling their spending habits as a means to building wealth.

Spending less doesn't mean deprivation. You can still enjoy all the finer things in life. They just need to be obtained in a more economical and financially planned way. In today's tough economy nobody can afford to overpay for necessities or luxuries. Once you master the art of reducing your expenses and consistently saving, there is no limit to your financial freedom.

The first step in evaluating your spending is to ask yourself, "Are the things that I'm purchasing wants, needs, or habits?" It's important to recognize any wasteful practices that have become habitual throughout your life.

Wants are things in our lives that we desire.
Needs are things that we have to have to survive.
Habits are things that we are used to doing.

This is how you recognize the difference and begin making the adjustments in your financial landscape. Take a piece a paper and track all of your spending in one day. Write down the name and cost of everything that you purchased in that one day. At the end of the day take another piece of paper and write across the top Wants, Needs, and Habits. Transcribe all the information in the appropriate category. Then you do the math. If the sum of the wants and habits category are each more than the sum of the needs category, then we have a problem.

Wants and habits usually are confused with needs based on individual interpretation. The difference is that they usually are accompanied by excuses and justifications. I think the rapper Jay-Z said it best, "Men and Women may lie but numbers don't." You might be able to fool yourself but you won't be able to fool the numbers on the bank statement.

Now ask yourself:

Am I an impulse buyer?
Am I often tempted by home shopping shows?
Am I tempted to purchase by television and on-line ads?
Am I lazy and just don't have time to look for the best deal?
Do I think about whether or not I really need something before I buy it?
Am I using good judgment, discipline and self-control when spending?

If these practices and behaviors sound familiar to you, no financial program will work for you. A lifestyle of excessive wants and habits will never lead you down the road of success. It will only lead you to ongoing financial instability.

I am guilty of all the above. I, too, for years exercised poor spending habits and my wants constantly won the battle against my needs. The light bulb went off for me when I was watching television one night and heard a Suze Orman the popular financial advisor say "If you wear it on your ass, it's not an asset." Wow!!! What a moment of revelation to realize that I had become a prisoner of things. Fortunately for me, I immediately starting reading any book of Suze Orman's that I could find. And, over time, I changed my thinking about money and my habits soon followed.

Avoiding Foreclosure

Unfortunately, many individuals are not on the verge of reaping the rewards of freedom. Whether it's poor budgeting, poor spending habits or just plain old bad luck, many individuals are on the verge of financial ruin. More specifically, bankruptcy filings and foreclosures in America are at an all-time high. And, I passionately believe that there is so much more we can do to help these individuals turnaround their financial situation. Much of my motivation for writing the Freedom Guide was with the goal in mind of helping more Americans keep their homes and their families secure.

It's very difficult in a foreclosure situation but there is hope. Trust me I understand. I really do. I've walked in the same shoes you're walking in. My primary residence had an auction date set. All that I had worked for seemed to be falling apart and quickly slipping away. It felt as though I was in the "Matrix" and that my life was moving in slow motion.

Going through foreclosure was a very frightening experience. I relied heavily on faith and a little ingenuity to pull me through.

This is how I gave birth to the Freedom Guide. And, it's also why I'm so passionate about my personal testimony and my desire to pass on the tools that I've gained to you help you, too, regain a sense of freedom in your life.

No one wants to lose their home, becoming another foreclosure statistic. But, every day more and more people are losing their homes. The Freedom Guide provides an alternative to just standing by and watching helplessly while you lose your home. The inconvenience of leaving your home for just a weekend seems like a small inconvenience to endure while having your mortgage paid in a weekend. As the saying goes, "Knowledge is power." the Freedom Guide provides you with a wealth of knowledge and a path to self-empowerment. But, it's up to you to begin using this knowledge to change your life circumstances.

If you currently are going through foreclosure, do everything you can to negotiate with the bank. Fully communicate with your mortgage company. Document and provide them with every detail pertaining to your financial hardship, medical challenges, reduced income, family issues and any other issues. The goal is to create a paper trail that supports your case for getting a loan modification and highlights all the circumstances that prohibit you from paying your mortgage.

There are many government programs and modification programs that you may be eligible for. Corresponding with your mortgage company will keep you abreast of all options available. You should specifically get in touch with their Home Retention Department.

Do not put your head in the sand regarding your delinquency. Make sure you read all correspondence. Being proactive and knowledgeable of your options and time constraints is major and will empower you in navigating the foreclosure process.

Successfully avoiding foreclosure sometimes is a war, not a battle. So, you have to think strategically to position yourself for the long haul. The Freedom Guide will provide you with additional income to fight the war. By following the "Seven Steps," you can immediately start working towards digging yourself out of the hole that you're in. There are no guarantees. But, as long as you maintain a positive attitude and apply the knowledge you have obtained, you'll at least give yourself a fighting chance.

There also are many advocacy non-profits and government agencies that can assist you with negotiating with your mortgage company. Seeking and finding some individual or organization to advocate for you is very important and provide you with an additional advantage in winning the war against foreclosure. If you can afford a reputable lawyer to intercede on your behalf, then, great. But, if you have to battle on a budget, then working with advocacy groups is a good recourse.

The rewards of freedom are not just monetary. It's more about giving. Because, it's through giving that our true rewards in life are multiplied. So next time you encounter a stranger, friend, family member, or co-worker that is going through a difficult financial situation, give them some words of encouragement and a copy of the Freedom Guide. It may be the lifeline they've been desperately searching for.

I would love to be one of the first to get the testimonial of how the vacation home rental business is working for you after having read the Freedom Guide. Please feel free to e-mail me at cathy@ FDGuide.com. I love success stories. There are tons of them flowing my way every day and I just love to hear about each and every one of them. It fills me with so much joy that the guide is changing lives every day. Each story may be different. But, we're all striving for one goal which is to have Peace of Mind. For those that are still working through the journey, know that success with the business is near and your commitment will result in a successful outcome.

A Letter to the Fan-Club

The *Freedom Guide* was born from trying times of financial turbulence in my life and in the lives of many others. In writing this book, I was enlightened. I learned so much about myself and my life purpose while also participating in the team effort of developing the 702vacationrentals.com website. Out of something that seemed so hopeless came something truly inspiring and a work that I'm truly proud of.

One of the biggest lessons I learned and greatest gifts I discovered is the power of laughter. You can't take the world's issues or yours too seriously. You just can't. Or, you run the risk of going nuts or developing medical problems. So, just laugh about it. As my fellow New Yorker's would say, "Forget about it." Put the energy in a positive direction. Let's stay healthy. "

I want to "thank you" for purchasing this guide. You took a risk and a chance that the Freedom Guide would benefit your household and your finances. And, it will. This little book will change your outlook, and if applied correctly, will change your financial situation.

I recently joined a local international church in Las Vegas. I have to give thanks to the congregation and the Husband and Wife Ministry team for helping me find my way. Being an entrepreneur has it challenges. But, I have a passion for business, and I love the art of closing a deal. I love the thrill of victory. Until recently, it's what I always thought I was born to do. Someone should have told me about the agony of defeat. Nevertheless, I've learned that my passion for business stems from my love of God, God's mercy, and my love for people.

I truly thank my family and friends, especially my mother. My mother has provided me with unwavering support for every million dollar idea that I've had since I was a kid. This is from selling lemonade at the Entertainers Classic Basketball Tournament (Rucker Park) in New York, direct sales of costume jewelry, and in and out of beauty salons in South West Philly.

No matter what, my mother has always supported me. She's always done simple things like giving me ice cream and cake when things didn't go exactly as I planned. But, we finally have a winner this time. So, thanks mom. You're a soldier, and I've learned from you to never ever give up hope.

It was hard for people around me to truly understand and see my vision. Some of my family and friends were perplexed. And, some days, I still don't think they get it. I guest when the repo-man knocks at their door they might ask me what this is all about. I guess I could say I was truly misunderstood.

The best part about it is that writing this book truly has been a labor of love. Many individuals have not been able to understand why I was writing this book. But, naysayers have actually motivated me to write this book. And, I'm still eager to convert them into an audience of believers. I want them to see that vacation home rental is a common sense idea that's worth a try, especially for individuals having financial difficulties. And, it's not like I started this thing. People have been doing this for decades long before I stumbled across the solution to my financial problems.

I also would like to extend a special shout out to a fellow entrepreneur Ms. Sandra Batiste. Our lives mirror one another's lives. And, the bar always seems to rise higher and higher each year. Thanks for your support. I'll meet you at Mike's Place in LaJolla for tea to celebrate the selling of the first 1 million copies. This time we'll wear white gloves and red dresses. Let's make a statement. In the words of my personal musical icon Diana, "I'm coming out. I want the world to know." I'm looking forward to the "pageant girl" and the "sorority girl" get together.

A special thanks to my good friend and fellow businesswoman Ada the motivator. You kept me going girl, and I'll never forget you. You passed "The Secret" on to me and God has now whispered it in my ear.

This guide is already a success. It rescued me from a low moment in my life. So, in retrospect, I'm grateful for being placed in that position. It enabled me to finally understand on a deeper level that when there's vision, there's provision. I finally understand LORD, and I now am listening more attentively.

This Guide was created for the public to utilize. And, helping others is the greatest success. So, make sure you tell others about the *Freedom Guide* so that we can keep the chain link of prosperity growing. Let's peel back the dark blinds of these financial strong holds, and let the sun shine in. Direct your friends to the website www.FDGuide.com. This gift of freedom will change their lives.

Thank You again and again for your support.

Author

Cathy Burch

References

Blanchard, Ken and Bowles, Sheldon. *Raving Fans: A Revolutionary Approach to Customer Service.* William Morrow and Co. 1993

Byrne, Rhonda. *The Secret.* Atria Books. 2006

Danko, William and Stanley, Thomas. *The Millionaire Next Door.* Pocket Books. 2010.

Gates, Sr. Bill. *Showing Up for Life.* Broadway Books. 2009

Gitomer, Jeffrey. *Little Red Book of Selling.* Bard Press. 2004

Karp, Gregory. *Living Rich by Spending Smart.* Pearson Education, Inc. 2008

Karpinski, Christine Hrib. *How to Rent Vacation Properties By Owner.* Kinney Pollack Press. 2008

Martin, Gail Z., *30 Days to Social Media Success.* Career Press. 2010.

Parnell, Anthony. *The Seven Laws of Stress Management.* iUniverse, 2008.

Vaynerchuk, Gary. *Crush It.* Harper Studio. 2009

Freedom Seminars

The Freedom Seminars feature guest speakers and experts covering a multitude of subject matters ranging from home retention, maximizing the income from your vacation home rental, staging, and internet marketing. For further information regarding Freedom Seminars and webinars visit www.fdguide.com or call toll free 1 (855) FDGUIDE. Mon-Fri 9am - 5pm PST 7days a week.

We welcome your feedback. Please send us an email at info@ fdguide.com.

Books Coming Soon by Author Cathy Burch

The Power of Positive Raindrops
www.positiveraindrops.com

The Adventures of the Pageant Girl and the Sorority Girl
www.psadventure.com

Sometimes I Cry at Night www.nightcrys.com

Closet Sleepers www.closetsleepers.com

All books will be available at all
www.MelrahBooks.com and retail outlets